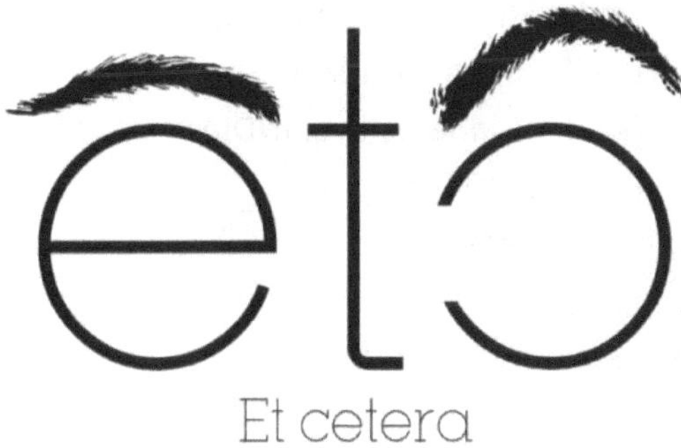

Et cetera

INDRANIL MUKHERJEE

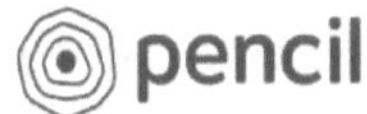 pencil

ISBN 978-93-5438-342-7
© INDRANIL MUKHERJEE 2020
Published in India 2020 by Pencil

A brand of
One Point Six Technologies Pvt. Ltd.
123, Building J2, Shram Seva Premises,
Wadala Truck Terminal, Wadala (E)
Mumbai 400037, Maharashtra, INDIA
E connect@thepencilapp.com
W www.thepencilapp.com

Author Biography

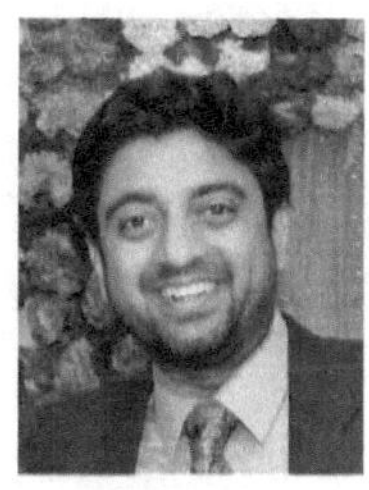

Indranil Mukherjee

Born in Kolkata, the City of Joy, Indranil had been keen on Art since childhood. He learned fine arts from the Birla Academy of Art and Culture for almost a decade, until he was compelled to leave the course for his Board Exams in 2001. However, his strong affinity towards sketching kept his dreams alive. During his college days in Bangalore, he was popular for penning temporary tattoos for his friends. His rooms remained decorated with vibrant paintings. Even today, while he travels outside the four walls, he often carries a small sketchbook to add life to some random lines on the go. For Indranil, Art is an inspiration to his happy times and a motivation to the tough ones. For him, art is simply a way of life. Besides fine arts, he got trained in a Digital Photography Certificate Course from Ram Krishna Mission Vidyamandira, Belur Math, Howrah in 2014. By this time, he, along with a few more like-minded artists, had founded VIBGYOR (www.infovibgyor.com) where art enthusiasts across the nation are indulged in various workshops to promote and pamper the passion. For VIBGYOR, learning is a continuous process, and sharing knowledge is even more important. The focus of the team VIBGYOR soon shifted to nurture and rejuvenate old, traditional art, many of which are on the verge of extinction today. VIBGYOR's new year (2021) calendar is a testimony to such efforts.

The lockdown in the recent past provided some additional opportunity to Indranil, which he utilized to reminisce and sketch some old memories from the snaps taken earlier. The journey was so satisfying, that he thought of making it larger, with this project.

Indranil is a Master's in Civil Engineering (Structures) with an Executive MBA from SPJIMR, Mumbai. Presently he is Assistant General Manager, Designs in an Engineering Consultancy firm in Navi Mumbai.

Reach Out

Contents

Preface

মুখবন্ধ

লেখক আমি কখনোই হতে চাইনি। আমি জানি সেই দক্ষতা আমার নেই। পেশায় আমি ইঞ্জিনিয়ার। আর নেশা হল ভারতের বিভিন্ন প্রান্তে ঘুরে বেড়ানো আর মন ও চোখ ভরে প্রাকৃতিক দৃশ্যের আনন্দ নেওয়া। আরও একটা নেশা হল নতুন মানুষের সাথে সম্পর্ক প্রতিস্থাপন।

সেই সব প্রাকৃতিক দৃশ্যাবলি বা মানুষজনের কীর্তিকলাপ কোনো সময়ে বন্দী হয়ে থাকতো আমার ক্যামেরার ভিতরে; কখনোও বা শুধুমাত্রই নিজের মনের মনিকোঠায়। 'Lockdown'-এর গৃহবন্দী জীবনে মনের অলিন্দে থাকা সেই সব ছবিগুলো বার বার উঁকি মারছিল। অলস সময়কে কাজে লাগিয়ে চেষ্টা করলাম মনের মধ্যে লুকিয়ে থাকা সেই সব চরিত্রগুলোকে পেনের খোঁচায় জীবন্ত করে তুলতে।

প্রত্যেক ছবির পিছনে একটা কাহিনী আছে। আর সেই কাহিনীগুলোর বেশ কয়েকটাতে আমিও যে অন্যতম চরিত্র। তাই পরে ভাবলাম অপটু হাতেই লিখব সে সব গল্প। যারা আমার আঁকা ছবি দেখবে, তারা ছবির পিছনের কথাটা জানবে না সেট হয়না। তাহলে কেমন যেন শিল্প অসম্পূর্ণ থাকে। আর শিল্পপ্রেমীদেরও মনের ক্ষুদা মেটে না।

সেই কারণে আপনাদের কাছে আমার এই সামান্য প্রতিবেদন। ছবির মধ্যে লুকিয়ে থাকা ঘটনাগুলো যদি আপনাদের ভালো লাগে তবেই আমার এই প্রয়াস সার্থক হবে।

এখানে আমি দশটা কাহিনী তুলে ধরেছি যার মধ্যে পাঁচটা আমার জীবনেরই অঙ্গ হয়ে আছে। আর বাকি পাঁচটির সাথে পরোক্ষ ভাবে আমি যুক্ত হয়েছি। সেই সব চরিত্রের পিছনের জীবনকথাকে উপলব্ধি করার চেষ্টা করেছি। আমার এই চিত্রকথা সমগ্রের নামকরণ করলাম- "ETC"। প্রাথমিকভাবে মনে হতে পারে কেন এই অদ্ভুত খেয়াল। আসলে এই নামের মধ্যেই সম্পৃক্ত আছে আমর সাধের দশটি sketch।
আপনাদের ভালোলাগাই হবে আমার চলার পথের পাথেয়।

ইতি
ইন্দ্রনীল মুখার্জী

Preface

I never longed to be a writer. Neither I possess the skill nor the ability. I am an Engineer by profession. My passion drives me to many lesser-known parts of India, where my eyes and mind get rejuvenated by the abundance of greenery and natural scenic extravaganza all around. Old architecture and traditional culture also fascinate me. So, meeting and knowing the people of my country became my favorite pastime.

Those glimpses from nature and human activities sometimes get captured through my lens and at other times, just within my mind.

During the prolonged days of captivity in 'Lockdown', these pictures were continuously haunting me. I decided to put this idle time to good use and started sketching those memories; mostly old, but some from recent times, as well.

Each sketch has a unique story as its backdrop. And I am also one of the active characters in a few of them... So, I thought of essaying the stories as well, even though I am an amateur in this trade. People, who will go through my sketches, have every right to also know their background. Otherwise, art remains unfulfilled, and the quest of the art-lovers, often under-satisfied.

That is why I have dared to make this humble submission. My efforts will be gratified if the story behind every sketch touches your soul and connects to the Indian culture at large.

Here, I have penned ten stories for the same number of skETChes. Out of these, five stories are an integral part of my life. And with the remaining five also, I am connected as a silent witness.

I have named this endeavor "ETC" i.e.Etcetera. Primarily, this name may seem to be weird. But when viewed from the perspective of an artist, all my ten sketches are woven around it!!!

Your love and patronage will be the sole source of my courage and energy to walk the miles ahead....

With warm regards -

Indranil Mukherjee

Acknowledgments

SPECIAL THANKS TO THE TEAM MEMBERS

Editor

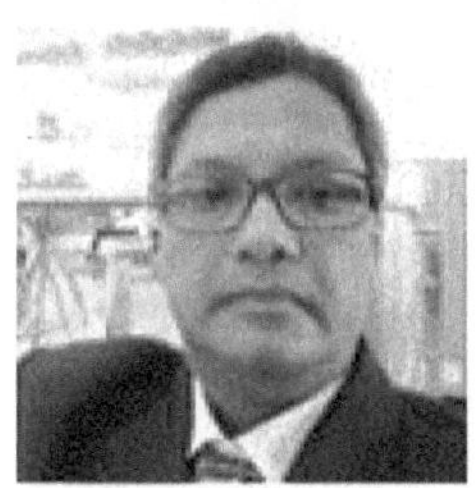

Amit Kumar Seal, *Kolkata*

By profession, Amit Kumar Seal is associated with an Engineering Major of international repute and manages the business for one of its construction verticals in India. I met him for the first time in the year 2012 as a colleague. But soon, we came close to each other, in personal terms. This was the time I started penning the travelogues and other write-ups on some of our heritages. I also did a few photo-documentaries on subjects ranging from traditional art to human culture. All these write-ups, whatever I have published to date, have been proof-checked by Amit Kumar Seal. He had the opportunity of residing amongst multi-cultural communities across India, which developed in him a truly modern and liberal personality. His thoughts are clear and realistic. His command over vernacular and official language has always provided the due crispness to the thoughts I have always wished to portray. It made me more and more confident as an essayist with time. Time has separated us geographically. But Amit-da still hand-holds me through his brilliant communication skill and unconditional love. This time as well, he is my obvious choice as an editor.

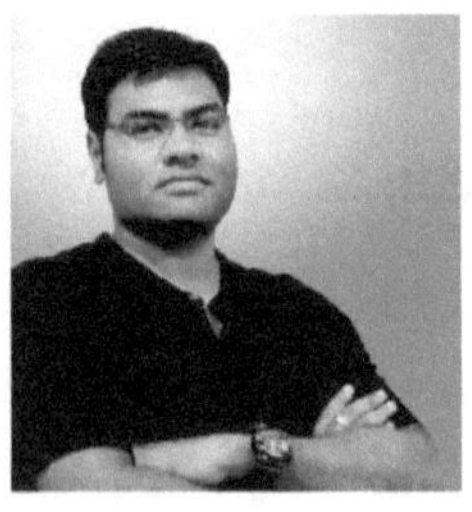

Creative Art Director

Mukkesh Sharma, *Hyderabad*

I was introduced to Mukkesh when he got associated with VIBGYOR in 2017. However, I met him in person for the first time when he traveled to Mumbai during the Group's photography exhibition in April 2019. Soon, we connected over common likings and approach towards genuine methodologies of creating art, especially photography. Professionally he is an Art Director in an Ad agency in Hyderabad and is also actively associated with ISKCON and UNDP-India for creative campaigns. He studied photojournalism at the New York Institute of Photography (NYIP). Presently, he is an active member of the National Press Photographers Association, America (NPPA) and Federation of Indian Photography (FIP), India. During the lockdown, I called him up to take his opinion about the project and he promised to help me. The name of this project "ETC" is a brain-child of Mukesh. This exhibits his sense of art, I could not have named this project better.

Chapter 1

Sole Story

"Bengal Professor thrashed for saving students."

Hindustan Times Headline, July 25, 2019

"The political scenario is now stable in India"- this has been always a myth, especially, when you are in a city like Kolkata.

During that time, I was deputed for a few months in the City of Joy for a specific project. The news of this Bengal professor was the topic of discussion across the city. Corporate offices were also not spared from this scoop of discussion. And in almost all these debates, the seniors raised the point of their good old student days for sure, when there were no such indecent happenings. Of course, we never argued on this point. But yes, irrespective of everything, this news was pretty disappointing.

Our office was just opposite to Maidan metro station, at JeevanDeep area. It is a part of the renowned Park Street zone of Kolkata, famous for tourist attractions, restaurants, bars, and lounges. Like every other day, that day also, three of us came downstairs after lunch to take a walk along the streets. While Sandip aimed to light a cigarette, Rudra and I opted for a sweet bite. I carried my laptop bag since I had to attend a client meeting, and wanted to take a cab after the short walk.

That day, the same old street wore a different look, as if the silence before a tornado. Every known face had anxiety, which neither they can bury, nor ignore, but just burn their skin. Just about 500 steps from the office building was a jewelry showroom. Right opposite to it, a cobbler used to sit at the edge of the pavement. Usually, whenever we cross this street, I have always found this cobbler active. There was someone or the other placing his foot on his wooden box to add shine to their boot. And this cobbler always used to be in a conversation mode, with a charming smile on his face. Sometimes, he used to look up to his customer's face for some response. But hardly he received any. That however, never stopped him from continuing his monologue.

Sandip and Rudra returned to the office after I booked my App Cab. I was waiting close to the cobbler and noticed my shoes may need a polish too. However, unlike others, I felt awkward to place my feet on the wooden box, right in front of his face. Instead, I thought of the middle way …

Hello.

Oh, hello Sir, you are alone today. Where are your two friends?

You have been following us till now?

Sir, what else do I have in life? I shine up boots and sit out here seeing the world around me in a rush. You don't smoke, like your other friend. That's a good habit. My brother lost his life, and all our ancestral property in his cancer treatment.

Oh, I am sorry.

That's ok Sir. Boot polish?

Ah… yes.

Normal, or special? Your attire today demands a special cream one. What do you prefer?

Ok, let's listen to the demand then.

Good choice. Keep your feet here.

No, I will take off my pair of boots, you do the job and then give them back.

Ok Sir, as you wish.

He opened up his pandora's box and took out three containers. He opened the lids and aligned them all in a row. Selected a brush from 3, and started dusting my left shoe first. All this time, he kept on talking to me. I was so engrossed in seeing his activity that I missed out on most of the conversation.

Sorry, what were you asking?

I asked, where are you heading for now?

For an official meeting, at BBD Bag.

You are an engineer?

Yes, how did you guess that?

That scientific calculator in your pocket, usually I see engineering students keeping them.

You have a pretty good observation I must say.

Thank you, sir, and my observation also says, this shoe needs serious attention. The sole is breathing its last.

I was shocked to hear that. I bent down to look close and tried to find any clue to this statement. I could hardly see anything beyond a mild crack. This also happened in my last pair of shoes. However, the pair could continue for another year before replacement.

This is a minor one, just ignore it. You better focus on the shoeshine.

Ok Sir, as you say. Where have you purchased this one?

In that handicraft fair, that was organized at Mohor Kunj last month. It's a new pair.

I see. I have a feeling that the shoe has been charged more than its actual cost. Most of these fairs do these tricks. You should rely on good brands and never compromise on shoes.

It suddenly struck my mind that this guy wanted to take me for a ride. First, those compliments to my attire, convincing me for a special polish; now, with a logical approach to replace the sole. But I had to prove myself smarter.

I have a meeting to attend, and I don't have time today. For time being you stick to the polish only. In case if something happens to the sole, I am here only, will come to you.

No no Sir, I understand your time is valuable. My intention was just to remind you about the steps that you place, after wearing this shoe. This shoe may betray you anytime. So be careful.

Ok ok, I understood. I will be careful.

By the way Sir, we have been conversing for so long, I have not asked you your name.

Indranil.

Wow, Lord Shiva, the sapphire, and the deep blue sky.

What?

Meaning...meaning of Indranil, sir.

Yes yes. And what's yours?

Sir, we don't bother so much with names. At my young age, villagers used to call me Pintoo. But parents had given me a name, Anmol Dash. Here, people just call me Polish.

As he kept on murmuring the story of his village, I took out the mobile from my trouser pocket and tried to check in the app, how close did my cab arrive. To my utmost surprise, even after 10 minutes, it's still showing 16 minutes to reach me. Is it at all moving towards my direction or not? As I kept focusing on the map, I realized the cab icon making some random turns, into some by lanes. I tried to connect the call to the driver, but it didn't reach out.

Sir your other pair?

Yes, take this.

Meantime please wear this pair of slippers. Else madam will get angry seeing the dirty socks.

Yes thanks, I was about to ask for it.

How far is your cab? Let me know, then I will speed up my activity. Sir, hardly anyone pays attention or responds to what I speak. After a long time, I am enjoying a conversation.

I have another 10-15 minutes. Don't know why the cab is not coming.

Oh, enough time for me to complete the polish.

Everyone seems a bit agitated in this area today. Especially the tea shop owner, and the public newspaper vendor. But you seem to be in a pretty good mood.

Sir this is how I am. My job is to clean with a brush and add shine. Someone got thrashed, at one corner of the city, unfortunately. It doesn't affect me. I will not be able to feed myself and my family if I don't continue my job. And, I believe, you should not do something that you are not enjoying.

So you enjoy boot polishing?

No sir, I enjoy conversing. I polish boots to meet new people. And earn a day's bread.

Who all are there in your family?

I have 3 kids. That's all.

And, your wife?

No sir, I am not married. Who will marry someone who talks so much?

I gave a blank look to him, and there was a pause. After the silence for a few prolonged seconds, he smiled and said.

Amar, Akbar, Anthony, my three kids, the street dogs. At the end of a day's work, I wrap up, buy some bread, then we 4 sit across this letterbox, and we have a happy family meal. Then, we talk to each other, sharing the entire day's experience and sleep here itself.

I was bowled over by the simplicity this man portrayed. Like, no obsession with status, money, lifestyle, but absolute pure and supreme happiness. Maybe, this is what Moksha means. Back in my mind, to some extent, I started to envy this side of Anmol.

Here you go, Sir. Look the way it's shining. Wear it, Sir.

How much?

Sir 20.

I took out a 50 rupee note and offered him.

You may keep the change.

Why sir, I need to pay back a change of 30 to you.

Yes, but, I am giving this tip to you.

Thank you, sir, my kids will also thank you. I will say Lord Shiva has sponsored the boiled eggs tonight.

And he raised his folded arms to thank me again. But, before I can even respond to that, there was sudden chaos heard from the end of the road. I bent across the pavement railing and found a huge mob approaching. They have their slogans written on huge placards and screaming on top of their voice. With curiosity, I quickly exchanged the slippers with my polished pair of shoes and observed the movement, trying to listen to the objective of this procession.

In Kolkata, such processions by blocking the traffic were not uncommon. The tea shop owner, the cobbler, the pedestrians, no one changed their course of action till then. But soon, they had to.

Police...run...!!!

Anmol quickly tried to wrap his belongings. When the chaos echoed from all corners of the street, I took no second thought but to run 500 steps, back to the safety of my office premise. I rushed inside the office building and screamed at the security.

Close the main gate, right now.

As he pulled the collapsible gate and locked them, I pressed the lift button hard, gasping for breath. Came upstairs, and rushed to the office terrace, which would give a clear view of the road from the 6th floor. As I looked down at the lane, I had a déjà vu. I had never seen such a scene before in real life. but in the movie Narnia, where the two teams had a clash across the battlefield. On one side, there were the students wearing handloom dresses, with placards and slogans, and on the other side were the police with their sticks.

Now I can relate to the reason for my cab taking odd routes. Even at this crisis, he didn't intend to cancel my ride, rather, he kept escaping. The network also played a game with both of us. Last night, a professor protested for the students and got beaten up by the political activists. But what is this agitation all for?

Soon things got even worse. The police aimed at the student protesters, but many innocent people got trapped in this roadblock. As they charged with their thick wooden baton, it failed to discriminate between students and other pedestrians. And in one such blow, I heard the thud on the tea stall shed. In that same clash, the gas oven toppled and it spilled fire. People started screaming and running all across, getting beaten up. What a mess is this? I questioned myself, are we civilized?

And to make this even worse, soon there were some media vans, which arrived for the live telecast of this chaos. By that time, the building terrace was full of my other colleagues. I was watching out of fear. Others were cross-checking their general knowledge.

I seriously don't connect to this political reasoning. Right from the beginning: thrashing a professor, repeating it, then student's violent protest, the police charging them. Are the police trying to stop the mob or add to the chaos? Who are the police supporting? The students or their political masters. The collateral damage to innocent people is just their misfortune to be in the wrong place at the wrong time.

After almost an hour, things seemed to have settled down for the time being. All commutes had been stopped, so everyone started discussing car pooling probabilities. I had a quick choice from Sandip, he stays very close to my apartment. Everyone started wrapping up fast before anything new erupts. As we headed downstairs, the entire group has formed subgroups talking in favor of or against the students, and a few are randomly changing groups to collect spices from the discussions. I was indeed feeling so left out.

As I stepped on the road, it's no more the same one that I visited an hour back. The deserted roads had only soft mourning from the innocent poor survivors, who had injuries waiting to be healed with time. Seeing one of them, I remembered about Anmol.

Sandip, take out your vehicle from the parking lot and meet me near the jewelry shop.

Why, what happened?

Just meet me there.

And I took some fast steps towards the letterbox. I could see Anmol sitting in that place, with one leg stretched wide. I reached out to him.

Are you ok?

He didn't speak. Didn't even look towards me. He kept one polish brush holding in his right hand. I can see his fingers trying to squeeze that brush. His broken jawbones also complimented the anger he was bearing inside him. He took out the 50 rupee note from his waist and gave it back to me.

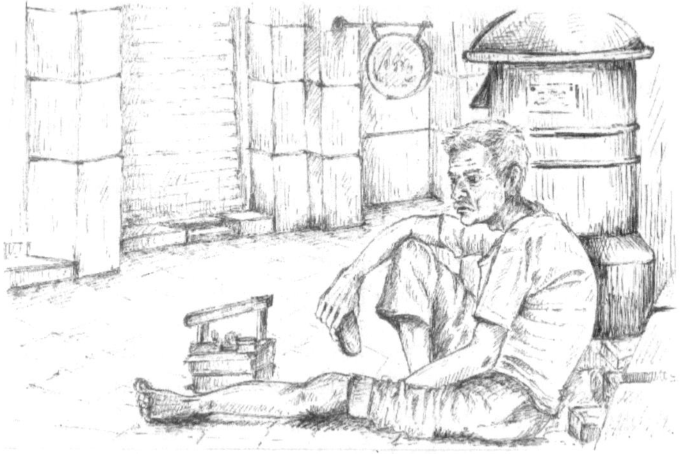

What happened?

I am homeless sir. They were beating me up too, trying to snatch my money and destroy my boot polish box. Anthony came rushing to protest and called for two of his brothers too. They left me aside and started beating the dogs. The burning stove from Ramesh-ji's tea stall spilled over Akbar, and seeing that the other two pounced to help him, but. They were not so lucky to have eggs tonight. And I don't need this money anymore. Please, Sir, take it back and go.

Anmol didn't even look towards me. But he kept his arms raised with the note until I took it back. I was at a loss for words, had no idea what to say. Before I can even think of initiating a conversation, a car honked.

Come on, what are you waiting for? We need to reach home fast before anything else starts.

Yes Sandip, coming.

I stepped inside the car, and it gushed across the deserted street. Sandip kept on talking about something, but my mind was blocked to receive anything. I took a deep breath and just stretched my body, arms, and feet. The left feet seem to flex much more than the right. What happened? That sole had sheared from the crack. But it's still shining from the top.

We didn't step on the right foot, I am sure…. !!!

Chapter 2

Performance Incentives

Yes, I have landed in Chennai, now I am heading towards my hotel. Ok, Maa, need to disconnect, I have just 2% battery left. Let me reach the hotel and call you back. Please inform Soumi, she may get tense if she finds my mobile switched off. Bye.

Sir, if you want to charge your phone, you may do it in my car during the transit time.

Oh, superb, that's a lifesaver.

Had to rush to board the flight for an official visit. I wonder why clients still insist on such personal meetings...!!! I mean, we are in the digital era, and the companies are investing a fortune in powerful internet, webcams, large displays, and whatnot? What are those investments meant for? Now, let's leave everything aside, it's time for me to gaze at the Chennai city life and observe the changes it has adopted since my last visit. Though I could hardly find any change from this cab ride, there is one thing for sure. It's almost a year since I have not met my dear friend Srivatsan. Time for a quick text message, and see if he can manage time for a cup of coffee. While the phone kept boosting its battery, I exhausted some of it to text him.

Hey, I am in Chennai. Landed some time back, and now heading towards the hotel. I am here for an official meeting tomorrow morning, and then, I have a return flight at 5 PM. You tell me how are you placed tomorrow? I planned to catch you up for coffee.

Srivatsan is always prompt to reply.

Hello brother. You have come for a very short time. But let's meet tomorrow morning. 5:30 AM at Marina Beach? That's the only possibility, seeing your day's schedule.

I am game for it.

After checking in, didn't waste much time or energy. Had some quick bite of dinner, and crashed out for an early wake-up. Morning alarms are always annoying. I face it daily. Even when it screams at 7:30 AM, I make sure I go for the snooze option at least thrice. But that day, even at 4:45 AM, the feeling was unlike a regular day. No idea from where this change in character happens. I was partially awake by 4:30 AM and was checking the mobile screen. So, that's human psychology. The excitement and first love, both kill a lot of good sleep even when you need it.

I booked a cab, which showed 15 minutes to Marina Beach watchtower. That's better, I was much before time. As I stepped out of the cab, I could feel the humid heat even before the sunrise. The strong LED lights have changed the color tone of my earlier memories of yellowish marina beach, to a whitish tone. But not just that, even the pathways across the locality have been made much tidy and neat. I preferred to get closer to the waves and stepped into the sand from the concrete roads. I could hear the waves lashing across the shore. However, the visuals were still partial. I walked rapidly toward them.

Across the horizon, I saw many colorful boats. It was time for the fishermen to come back with a good catch. Few had arrived already and others were heading back. I took out the mobile to take a quick snap of the same. The sun was peeping from the horizon, and it was such a pleasant start for the day. As if, all my fatigue just got washed away in its serenity. With the mobile in hand, I realized I was there to meet someone. Where is Srivatsan? Dialed his number to check.

Where are you? I am standing at the shore, in front of the Watchtower.

Yes, I am on my way. Will be there in another 15 minutes.

Ok, then just call me once you reach here. Meantime, let me enjoy a walk along the beach.

Yes sure.

As I walked towards the southern end, I chose to hold the slippers in hand and let the waves come and wet my bare feet. It's a common human favorite, and a proven relaxation technique. But beyond that, it's childish to kick those waves as it comes within the reach of the feet.

While I was engaging myself in such pleasures, I looked around for the morning activities happening around me. There was a group of stout gymnasts doing exercise. One leader was guiding the team of another 10, who were monitored for the short run and a vault over the sand. In the background, there was some old generation group who were forcing themselves to laugh their heart out. Laughter is also mocked these days, and you need to put effort to generate it.

As I gazed at those activities and walked a few yards more, I found a fisherman sitting beside his boat and segregating the catch for the day. He seemed to have been talking to someone. I could not understand a word that he spoke, but I understood that he was in some conversation. But there was no one around him. I have seen a similar scene. when Ravi Prasad sir, our site PM, had bought his first Bluetooth microphone. It's very awkward indeed to find someone talking to an imaginary person without holding the phone in hand. I thought maybe in a similar way, this fisherman is also hooked to some technology. I took further interest to investigate the matter and casually made a brisk walk across the person and his boat. No, I could barely see any device for communication. Then he might be talking to himself, I concluded.

But besides that, more interesting was the way he was separating the fish and the crab that got stuck in the net, and made the web ready for the next catch. The types of fish were segregated based on category as well, as they were taken out from the wired situation. One interesting fact, the cats were in very close proximity but were not in the mode to pounce on the fresh fish stocks. This was unusual. I was curious and inquisitive too. The fisherman, the fish stock, the fishing net, the boat, and the cat, rather a kitten. Something was cooking up, which I felt urged to investigate and understand.

The kitten was young and energetic, and over to that, even smart. It observed the fisherman very carefully, and whenever he got engaged in solving complicated ties of the web, that's the time when it would start taking small steps towards the fishes. Absolute calculated baby steps, and very careful body movements. It was almost reaching out to its target when came the third character of this drama…Enter the black crow. This entry was no less than that of a South Indian hero, in a commercial movie. Hardly anyone had a clue from where it appeared.

The crow took a small elevated flight from the sand horizon and braked in front of the approaching cat. More than the flight quantum, the wings were flattered so strong that the kitten got surprised and felt threatened. With a few steps back, the rebellious kitten tried to roar like a tiger, but it all faded in the ambiance with the breeze. The crow now leaped further to the kitten with absolute silence, as if it's offering an open challenge. The kitten, who found his size not fit for a confrontation, slowly moved back a few more steps.

Super cako...!!!

The fisherman smiles at the crow and exclaims. He then finds a small fish from the collection and throws it towards the crow. The crow now makes a prompt flight to catch it in the air. What a catch !!! Reminds me of Jonty Rhodes. The crow took the fish tightly in its beaks, and then took a safe landing on the boat to feast on it. And the fishermen started murmuring again.

Now, I could understand the communication cycle. All this time, the fisherman was in conversation with the crow only. The crow was happy with the prompt incentive for the job done. To please his master, it even started nodding to a few of the comments from the fisherman. One should seriously look at the expression of

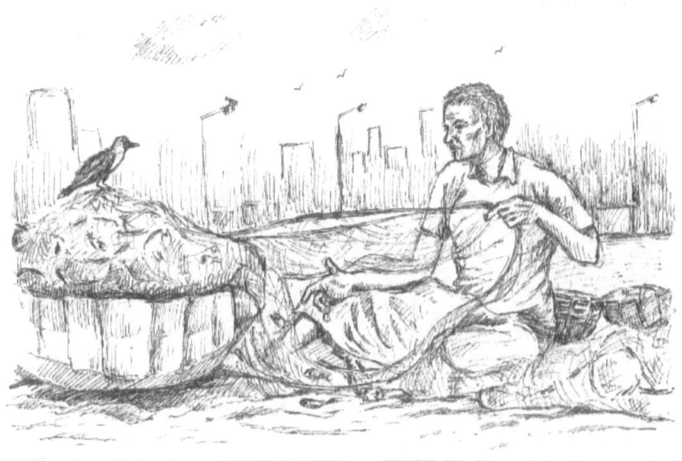

the kitten then. It seemed as if it was accumulating all the curse it could, to shower them all on that one crow. Its blue eyes turned sharper and a silent roar again, just to make the point, the game is not over yet. The fisherman was absolutely in trance, where he kept on talking, smiling, all by himself, as if the crow was responding to him. At times, he might have even commented on behalf of the crow by himself as well, just to keep the conversation going. I wished I could have understood Tamil, to relate to the conversation even more. The mobile rang right at that very moment.

Hey buddy, I have reached, where are you?

Sri, just walk towards your left along the beach, I am close to the first boat that you see after the Beach Yoga group.

Ok, I will be there.

I was not willing to compromise even a second of this wonderful sight. Now that Sri was there, I was more excited to get the conversation translated. We greeted each other with a tight hug. It was indeed a pleasure meeting Sri after a long time. We had a quick exchange of words, soon after which I asked him to translate what the fisherman was saying. He started paying attention too, to this ongoing activity and the fisherman's conversation. And within no time, he started chuckling.

Hey, translate, what's so funny?

This guy is talking his heart out to the crow. He is calling it Cako, which means brother.

Ok, what's the conversation?

He is saying everything...like, he wanted to have crab last night, but his son-in-law came and asked for chicken biryani. His wife didn't cook crab and they both fought. Mistakenly he spilled the rice bowl, for which his wife had beaten him up with a broomstick. Hey, this man is confessing his sorrows of life to the crow. This is funny.

Does the crow understand?

Well, he now says, no matter what happens, he loves his wife.

As Srivatsan was translating and laughing in succession to one another, I noticed the kitten getting charged up for the next attack. And the crab tentacles are making the man busy to save the wired net. The responsible crow was now keeping the ears for the master and its eyes on the trespasser, waiting for the right time to defend. The moment the kitten steps inside the dangerous orbit, the crow takes its flight again, to prevent the invasion. The same silent rival pushed back the kitten to its start point. The crow flared the wings before it turned around. As if it just raised the shirt collar to prove his victory. The fisherman was happy again. Once again, he finds one small fish to appraise the crow and releases it towards the "loyal employee".

This, I presume, is the most honest appraisal I have ever come across. Absolute 100% performance-based incentive and the rewards are promptly given, without any delay. Also, I have never seen such a committed boss, who likes to keep things transparent with the employee and maintains his promises without any reminder put forward. The crow also kept his performance consistent. It didn't just make the fisherman work in peace, but it also helped him to pour his heart out without fear. The ecosystem set around this one boat was balanced. The only one who felt deprived was the kitten. That's because the kitten was always aiming for the bigger fishes, which were caught for sale in the market.

As I was appreciating this employment, I remembered that my previous year's performance incentive was yet to be credited. Even after making the best efforts last year, my management made the same stereotype comment, " IT WAS GOOD, BUT IT COULD BE BETTER." And they forced upon me with a much lesser incentive than what I deserved. Now, that too is pending!! The flow of thoughts could not ring more into my mind... It's my Boss calling... !!!

Chapter 3

Folklore

Hey Vinod, seems like your boss is on leave today, calling me in the peak working hours on a Wednesday... I hope everything's ok?

Yes, all's well. I called up to wish you on your Special Date.

But I don't have any occasion today.

Last month on the same date, we danced our hearts out, while you were busy taking the life-time oath with Soumi. Congratulations buddy, on one month of marriage.

Ahh, thanks. But, you know, I am seriously repenting the leave taken before the marriage rather than extending it on the other side.

I still think you have a chance to extend on the other side as well.

No way, ever since I have re-joined the office, it's going crazy at work. I am yet to plan our honeymoon. Every day as I reach home, I need to keep a backup excuse ready to divert this discussion.

You may always plan for it. What's the big deal?

What ??? !!!

Okay, let me first understand; given a chance, where will you opt for a honeymoon?

Maybe Shimla, it's a good season now. Or Rajasthan. Soumi has more affinity for the latter.

Does she like a camel?

No, not that way... But she is fond of folk music. There is an annual folk music festival in Rajasthan this month. But this plan will need at least a ten day's leave, which I am not in a position to even ask for.

I see. Well, then I have a different suggestion for you... A plan that would fulfill your wishes; a plan which enables you to rejoice and not repent; a plan which requires the least intricate planning...

What?

If she likes folk music, and that you are in Kolkata now, there is an option in just a few hour's drive from Kolkata... in the land of folk music, the sweet place of serenity; the soil of our respected KaviguruRavindranath Tagore.

You mean Shantiniketan?

Of course. Every Saturday, there is a beautiful festival-type gathering across the open space, at the banks of the Kiwai river. There you will get live Baul music and handicraft fair. I even know Chitra-di, who curates this entire gathering.

That's interesting. I am sure Monday's stomach upset excuse will be enough to place this plan across the coming weekend.

Yes for sure. I am sending Chitra-di's number. Give my reference. And go for it.

Thanks. And you better get back to work. Bye.

Vinod was right. Many a time, there are things equally beautiful and praiseworthy right in front of us, but we always end up aiming for the farthest one and then regret the inability to reach it. This was indeed an ideal example of one such foolishness. Soumi loves folk music, she has not clarified she wants specific folk music of Kutch. Shantiniketan indeed was not a bad idea at all.

Shantiniketan, the name itself has the word Shanti, meaning peace. It's in the neighborhood of Bolpur, in Birbhum district, West Bengal. And from Kolkata, it is just a few hours by train. So there is no booking headache in this plan. We only need to board the train. And I was sure that Chitra-di would have suggested the same. All these things were weaving the urge for the weekend gateway to Shantiniketan, when it got pampered by a phone blink... the contact details of Chitra-di. Without any further delay, I dialed the number.

Hello is it Chitra-di?

Yes, who's this?

I am Indra, from Kolkata. Vinod's friend.

Oh yes, he texted me about you. So you are planning to come this Saturday morning?

Yes, that's what I was thinking. I will come along with my wife. She is yet to be informed about this, but I think she will be equally excited about this.

You both are most welcome. You may stay at my cottage itself. I will clean a special room ready for you both.

That will be a great help for sure. I was about to ask you for this help. You made my day. Well, any advance payment?

No, not required. See you both on Saturday morning.

Thanks, Chitra-di. See you.

On the following Saturday morning, Soumi and I boarded the passenger train from Sealdah station. The crowd in that route was fortunately in control, and we managed two seats for our 3-hour journey. We got down at Bolpur station. It had been a long time since I had traveled on a passenger train in West Bengal. That's indeed an experience of its own. We took a cycle rickshaw parked right at the exit of the station. Chitra-di seems to be quite a famous lady in the locality. As soon as I mentioned her name, the rickshaw puller didn't even ask for an address clarification.

We both took the seat, and the rickshaw wala started paddling his vehicle. As we passed a few yards away from the station area, I felt the aura of the place engaging my soul. There was no rush across the streets, as if, this is a part of the Utopian World. People all around us seemed so happy and content. Everyone was so much basked in the divinity of Tagore, that even the tree trunks seem to have creative postures. As if they are in one of the mudras of Bharatnatyam. Very soon, I found that the concrete roads have transformed into red soil. It seemed as if we have left the catastrophes far behind, and going more deeply into nature.

And without any hiccups, the rickshaw driver rode us to Chitra-di's place. The cottage was no less than any mansion. There was a huge open platform at the entrance, at the end of which, there was a framework of the Durga idol kept, which indicates the ritual of Durga Puja in that place.

Welcome Sir, welcome Madam.

Hello Chitra-di.

Saheb, I am not Chitra-di. I am the caretaker of this cottage.

Oh, sorry. What is your name?

Savitri.

Ok, where is Chitra-di?

You may meet her in the evening. She is busy now with today's fair arrangement.

Ahh, that's the highlight of the day. So where does that take place?

Saheb, right here, this entire area outside this cottage. By 4 PM, you will find this place transformed into a full-fledged festival.

Wow, anxiously waiting to see it. Fine then, let us get fresh, have some food, and preserve some energy for the evening party.

Yes, Saheb. Please come, let me show you your room.

Though it was a bright sunny day, the abundance of trees and greenery in that locality made us feel pretty comfortable outdoors. We freshened up, had a sumptuous brunch, and strolled around. I engaged myself in taking some clicks as well, balanced with serene nature and human portraits of tribes from nearby villages. The cottage of Chitra-di was also equally mesmerizing, where Soumi posed for some of her traditional social media display picture collection. No matter what we did, both of our minds were revolving around the same anxious wait for the clock to tick past 4 PM.

And, Savitri-di was right. That evening when we stepped outside the cottage, that entire place was so different. The entire area was filled with a chirpy gathering, with tribal artisans selling all sorts of handicraft products. From small showpieces made of metal to handloom apparel to creative lampshades and lamps. Everything was looking so colorful and artistic. And with such colorful visuals of art making a solid benchmark, the ambiance was built up stronger with the background score of some folk songs, which traveled to our ears from the surrounding. The sound was natural, not amplified mechanically, and no matter which part of the fair you stand, you are bound to hear one of those songs enriching your experience. What a wonderful planning and arrangement!

This rustic folk music experience was created live by various groups of Baul. Each group was occupying a shade of a huge tree, maintaining a minimum distance from each other. We just randomly chose to reach out to the nearest tree shed. As we went closer to the tree, that song started amplifying to us naturally, and I got engrossed in its words more. I could see the man singing the song. He was in his vermilion robe, and wore a turban, playing a 3-string instrument. His performance was extremely natural and that filled up space all around that tree, creating a heavenly ambiance. The blend of his rustic voice and the soothing tones from the strings created a wonderful melancholy. It almost hypnotized me, and I plunged deep into the words he sang...

Dekho bhalo joney roilo bhanga ghorey,

Mondo je shey shinghashoney chorey

It means that the ones who are good to society and choose to go by the honest route of life, are residing in worn-out or broken shelters. On the other hand, the one who chose the indecent, dishonest, and unethical path, rises to the helm of power and authority. The song was known to me, I remember I have heard this song in a movie by lifetime Oscar Winner Satyajit Ray. But then, I was too young to understand the meaning of the words. Today, the same words played differently in my mind. As if, it was forcing me to open my eyes and see a naked truth dancing in front of me.

Shonar foshol folay je tar,

Dui bela jotey na ahaar

The one who toils across the fields across his life, the farmers, they hardly get to feed themselves or their family members; not even the bare minimum required nutrition is met. But still, they don't give up. They, and their generations thereafter, are dedicated to farming and make room for all others in society to be fed.

With every line he sang, I started connecting myself to the hard realities of life. It's like something we all know, but we tend to ignore it. We always keep prioritizing our life with trivialities. But we tend to ignore the ones which make larger impacts. We say, we are a part of society, but actually, the truth is, we are just for ourselves, and selfishly living our life.

I took a pause and went back into my life for a few years. My priority was to book a movie ticket and I got irritated for not fetching a ticket in the reclining chair. Maybe by then, someone somewhere in this farmer's family must have lost his or her life due to malnutrition. I aimed to get admission to a good engineering college. And I was a bit upset about not getting a seat at a prestigious university in Kolkata. Maybe by then, a farmer must have started teaching his son to plow and water the seeds. While I was busy comparing the Mac Donald's meal schemes, on the other corner in this world, there was someone who was picking up the leftover food from the dustbin to feed himself. Life is so unfair, unbalanced...and we humans are so selfish. We just don't see the bigger picture.

Kotoi rongo dekhi duniya-e

Life...so many colors to see...indeed true!

By the time the song ended, I already had a short tour of self-realization. Took a deep breath. We always tend to take, and we are not open to give. This is common human psychology, which has evolved the discount coupon concept in marketing. The same product, with a high MRP, and a petty discount charms you more, than a stable MRP and fixed pricing. And we bargain when we buy something. That saving doesn't benefit much to the buyer but affects the seller, especially when they are honest artists like the people around us in that fair.

Listen, the Baul sang so well, I think we should offer him something.

He just didn't sing, he displayed the life canvas. Yes, let's do this.

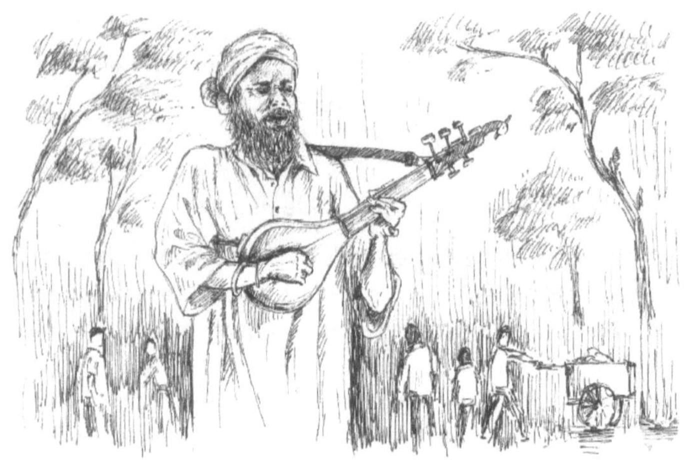

I realized, just like me, even Soumi had some life lessons learned out of this performance. We stepped forward towards the Baul. Many like us came forward to offer some money, as a note of thanks and appreciation. And the Baul was accepting it, with folded hands and a bow to convey thanks. But, he never demanded anything from anyone. Many even walked past, after they had recorded the song, or made their social media live. As we headed closer, I saw, most of the offered denominations are 10 rupee notes at their best; mostly coins. He didn't show any greed, nor demand. This is one more problem with many of us, we don't value Art to the extent it should have been. I felt bad, and with all the guilt that the realization gave to me, I opted to offer a five hundred rupee note. Seeing the amount, the Baul took a pause and looked up to me. He smiled at me, folded his hands, and bowed again. As a cultural gesture, I followed doing the same.

I am glad you felt the song. Others just listened.

No, but you sang too well.

It's not the song, it's the reality and the realization. Everyone cannot bask in the truth of life, it needs maturity, not of age, but the mind. Saheb, I am indeed sorry, but I cannot take this money.

Why? What's wrong with taking this money? I am offering it from my wish, I loved the performance.

Saheb, I have a very limited requirement. There is a daily quota of income which I keep, and once that is achieved, I don't sing anymore for the public. I go deep into the woods and spend time with nature, and practice. If I take this amount, my requirement for this evening will be over fulfilled, and I will not sing anymore.

It's ok, you may take this and continue singing.

No sir, rather, you listen to one more song. And give this to someone who needs it more than me.

I was shaken by the gesture and purity of thought. I could not argue with him further. Across our lives, we keep running after achievements, which are mostly measured in terms of hard cash accumulated. And we judge people and their success accordingly. This person has so little in comparison, but still, he was so enriched by himself, so happy, contented, successful, and determined in life. Maybe, I will never tell my HR to reduce the increment offered to me at the end of the performance year.

I had no ground for argument with him, and I couldn't take the blame to stop the performance of the evening as well. I smiled, and agreed to his request, and stepped back to take another lesson of life. The Baul made one more impactful presentation of ground reality with a rustic voice and words piercing the heart. Indeed, *Kotoi rongo dekhi duniya-e...*

Shall we now check out the handicrafts a bit? I want to buy some earrings matching the peacock green color saree that your aunt from Kakurgachi has given me at our wedding.

Yes, let's go. But, promise you won't bargain.

Chapter 04

The Finishing Line

The Royal Calcutta Turf Club, RCTC, had been doing rounds on my mind for years. I decided to end this long-time curiosity with a final semester project for my Photography Course. All necessary permissions were taken in advance, so that I can stick to my plan even with the toughest deadline. And finally, that day clocked ….

It was an immense fortune to me, that the Derby was also scheduled during that weekend, and the administration was hyperactive. The security was tighter than regular. As I approached the main entrance, there stood a tall stout security guard. I showed him my credentials. All my email communication was with Mr. AnitCasyab, whom I have never met. The guard asked me to follow him to the office room, and on our way, we luckily found the person.

There goes Casyab Sir. Talk to him first, and then do as he instructs.

I found a handsome man in his mid 40's, carrying his attitude perfectly in his dark blue suit over a pink shirt.

The gelled hair combed backward was set enough to handle a horse ride. And the sharp-pointed fancy brown shoe was adding more glamour to the showbiz. The guard introduced me to Mr. Casyab, and he recollected our conversation promptly.

Ah yes, so you are the photo enthusiast. See buddy, I don't want any trouble or complaint. It was tough to convince the management of your plea, especially for the Derby. You need to make sure that it doesn't burn my fingers.

No Sir, I won't allow anything of that sort.

Cool !!! I feel this is your first time within racecourse premises. Next time onwards, to access the member's area, make sure you are in absolute formals and leather shoes. No casual dressing is allowed in that lobby.

Sure Sir, I deeply apologize, I was unaware of this.

No issues, today is just a practice day. Have a look around, and then the main race is on this Saturday morning. That day, there should not be any excuses.

Noted, Sir.

This guard will take you around the premises. Before you leave today, collect a formal letter, and carry that along within this premise on Saturday. And this guard will also tell you which boundaries you should not trespass. Have a good day.

The strict introduction made me more conscious. I realized this is a serious business, and I need to put my steps carefully. I increased my questions to be asked to the guard, who never got bored to answer me. I scanned the entire place and scanned the map for my positions for the race day. After all foolproof checks, I collected the letter and went back...anxiously waiting for the main day.

Saturday, I didn't want to miss a single moment. Right from the betting book being sold outside, to the bets being placed, I wanted to document every moment. This time, I was dressed exactly the way I would have for any upcoming interview. I know my boundaries, and I was happily taking my shots. Suddenly, I heard my name being called. It's Mr. Casyab.

Good morning Sir.

So, you are already in your roles. I may probably not have been seen around, as I will be doing the commentary for the race. But I guess you already know the rules for this arena. All the best, take good clicks. Do share with us as well.

Before I could even respond, I heard announcements. The horses with assigned riders are now making a public display, and by seeing that, the bookies are confirming the bets, or changing them. After that, the jockey slowly rode their horses towards the start line. No one is allowed at the start line, so now, everyone goes back to their seating positions. I had permission to enter the members' lobby and so I did.

This place was so well maintained. The wooden seats are polished and numbered. The walls were painted and there were TV screens almost at each corner. And the finish line is best viewed from here, exactly at a perpendicular angle. I was so excited to see the first real-time horse race of my life. I could not follow the terminologies that Mr. Casyab said across commentary, but I waited for the starting signal. There was a big screen where the live-action was being telecast.

There was an absolute silence before the start, and I could even hear the breeze blowing. And on the count of three, goes the start signal with an air-gun shot. Immediately, I sensed a tension growing all across the field. The horses were seen across the big screens. The race had already started. As the horses raced along the track, I could sense the tension moment too, even though I had not set any bet for them.

As the horses approached the finish line, I found the scream from the other side of the lobby going high on its pitch and volume. That's the lobby for non-members. And before I could sense what was happening, there was Mr. Casyab congratulating horse number 3 for winning the race. Everything happened so fast. I got lost and confused.

I approached one old man sitting alone in the member's lobby, and looking at BOL, the betting book.

Sir, is the race over? I mean, no more race?

He pulled his cigar out of his mouth and scanned me from top to bottom.

First day?

Sir, I am here just to shoot some photos.

Ahh... See my son, the race has just started. One race is over. Now everyone will move outside and place the bet again. There will be a display of the assigned jockey with respective horses, and then, the next race. It's a derby, the races will continue for quite some time.

Oh, that's wonderful. One more thing. The lobby on the other side seems to be highly energetic. Here people are watching the game with so much calmness.

That's because we are educated, but mind you, we are not calm as well. As soon as the horses start galloping, we see our bets galloping too. It's just that, we have control over emotions. This is an exclusive member's area. The hooligans shouting from the other end are commoners and non-members.

Oh, I see. So, are you not betting anymore?

I have my person at the counter to place the bet. I have texted him my next bet.

Thanks, may I take a photo of yours?

No, please, no photographs.

That gave me all the clarity. Here, if I seek permission for a portrait, I will be denied. So, I have to go far and use a tele lens for a candid shot. Also, I understood that the race is a matter of just 10 seconds or a maximum of 15, but there are so many elements running parallel. I understood that I have to divide the tasks for each content. So, I saw the time table, that there are more than 10 races to go. And I secured one aspect to be properly covered for each upcoming race. Apart from all this, there were some nice live performances and eateries arranged for refreshment, especially for those who have come to enjoy, not to bet.

This plan was showing a fruitful result of my documentation. I started focusing on subjects. The allotment of the jockeys, the display march, slow gallops of the horses towards the starting line, all well secured. Then, I had to focus on the race images. I was back at the member's lobby for the same.

For each race, I shifted my location from one spot to the other, experimenting with angles and the settings of the camera. It was indeed quite an experience and learning. I even took a few shots of that old man while the horses were about to reach the finishing line. That was the moment when I had a change of perspective.

I recollected the words of the old man, who said it right, as the horses gallop on the race track, the spectator's heart starts running fast as well. And it speeds up as the horses' inch close to the finishing line. It was not just the jockey who rose off the saddle to fetch the maximum throttle to the end line, but the spectators also were at the edge of their seats to match the rhythm of the race. That one line was decisive of profit and loss, win or loss. As soon as the race was over, few took their seats again and made phone calls with a smile on their faces. That meant, it's a win, and he was asking his person to bet for more into the next race. Few sat back, but with a bang, and even hit their armrests with folded fists. They too made calls and asked their persons to bet for a new horse or jockey. The neutral reactions were from people who didn't bet. They just loved the color of the horses and the adrenaline rush at the finishing line. Yes, they too made phone calls, to order a bottle of beer. However, there was an air of sophistication all around. This was all about the members' lobby stretching through five races. Then, I thought to be one among the common men.

I stepped into the common lobby. Well, no doubt, things were pretty different. It was a different world altogether. The seats were not so well maintained, and not at all tidy and polished. It was meant to be seated, and that's all. But the number of people was much more than the other side. Many were smoking and littering all around.

I found a very old man again. This person was wearing a white kurta, that had turned close to light maroon by then, and a striped lungi. The slippers were also not in very good condition. I wondered, how can this man bet in a Derby race? This person can hardly even feed himself or his family. I took some courage to approach him and initiate a discussion.

Kaka, what do you think? Who is going to win this one?

The old man turns to me and smiles. I could count his remaining three teeth, which were too coated with the excess consumption of tobacco. He pulls out a bidi from his ear and lights it up. He released the smoke up in the air as high as he could and coughed twice in return. Then, he showed me three fingers and exclaimed

Three...horse number three, my lucky number.

How much have you bet?

In the first race, I started with 10 rupees. By now I have won 2000. So, This time, I have put 500.

That's good. All the best.

How much have you bet?

No kaka, I am here just to click images.

Then take my photo too.

And he gave a pose holding the bidi with his right hand and the BOL betting book in his left. I clicked.

The contrast of characters between the two old men at the two opposite sides of the race-course was obvious.

By then, the horses were at the starting point. Mr. Casyab has started commenting about the technical specifications of the horses and the assigned jockeys, and their statistics. As soon as the race started, the mob walked closer to the fence. This was so very different from the member's lobby. People started screaming on top of their voice, a few called for the gods, few called names of their horses and the jockey to motivate them, others even screamed foul languages. The entire energy of this common area was raw and rustic.

The horses are again on the racing track and they are heading towards the finish line. The excitement reaches its epitome with every second it passed by. And as soon as the race reached its culmination, some hopes were built and broken simultaneously. On this side, there was none to just observe and sip the beer. They were all players in the game.

Kaka, what happened? Did you win?

No, this time was a miss. But, I won't give up. There are still 3 more races to go. I have promised to make 5000 today.

Why that specific figure?

My son is in the hospital. The authorities have given a deadline for the charges to be paid by tonight, else, they won't continue the treatment.

Oh, I am sorry. But, what if you lose?

We don't have much to lose, so we never worry too much about that. God is there, I will win for sure. This time 1000.

I could realize the tension was much more than just a bet to win or lose. It was in concern for someone's life as well. I decided to continue my shoot from the common area for the last few matches. I shifted my positions to grab some moments from different perspectives. But my focus was stuck to Kaka. I found him still smiling and chatting with other people around him, but, as soon as the race started, he was numb, and constantly puffing the bidi.

The last race of the day...As Mr. Casyab announced over the microphone. Everyone got some extra time to recalculate all their money and play the best bet. Kaka was calm and quiet. I didn't intend to disturb him in his mental calculations. People started placing their bets and rechecked the receipts. Everyone was set to try their luck for the last time for that day.

As the race started, everyone was on their feet. No one was found seated except very few, who were old enough to stand for long. People with folded hands and cross fingers leaned forward. Few took out the christ locket and started kissing it. One person started chanting the Hanuman Chalisa. Crazy things all around. But as thehorses were in front of the eyes, it seemed, the world had

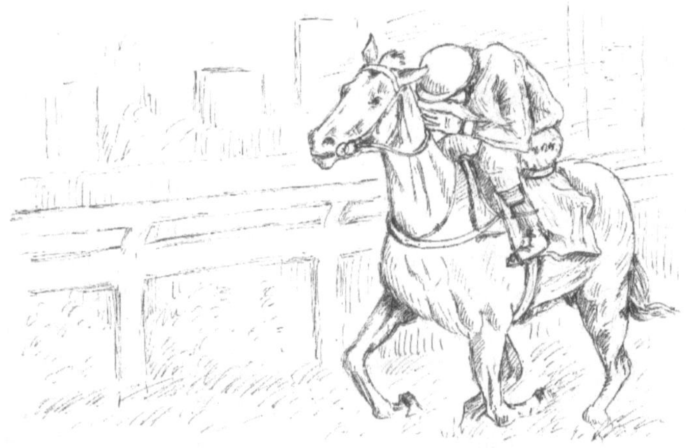

slowed down. Like a slow-motion movie, I could hear nothing but severe heartbeats and running sweat. Everyone was at a loss of emotion but focused on their bet. With the betting receipt squeezed tight in the fist, they exclaimed to push their luck to their respective victory.

With the finishing line, all these emotions burst out together. A blend of happiness of win and sorrow of loss, all under the same roof. And everyone expressed the match in their way. I quickly managed to capture a few moments. But then, I realized, Kaka is missing from the crowd. I tried to trace him and finally found him standing at the exit passage. The horses after the race are now being taken back from this area. As soon as horse number 3 was about to pass by, Kaka tore the BOL booking booklet and threw it at the jockey. I understood it was not a fair game for him.

My phone rang, and it's Mr. Casyab.

Where are you, buddy?

Sir... Still on the grounds.

So, how did it go?

I bet, much more than I expected.

Chapter-5

The Taproom Bar

Oh, no…It's pouring heavily outside.

So what? The first monsoon. Let's enjoy this evening. And it's good we have a non-working Saturday tomorrow. So, a long weekend.

Guruprasad could convert any situation in life into a reason to indulge upon sloth. At times, I seriously ponder how every agenda or activity can target one final solution, alcohol. Well, maybe that's his way of enjoying life. A democratic country gives every individual his choice. I don't know whether that even allows him to puke upon Sachin's new bed sheet on the day of his house warming ceremony.

Perhaps, that's why Sachin looked into the lift mirror, pretending as if he didn't hear anything. But as the digits on the display panel started diminishing, my choice for the evening had vanished. By then, Guruprasad had already succeeded, to convince me for the Taproom Bar.

Come on yaar, I know you won't drive your bike in this heavy downpour. You are prone to cold. And this weather change is too horrible. The new bar is just a stone's throw distance from here.

But how to reach out to that place even?

Sachin is coming with us in his new car.

No guys, please spare me today, I have to rush. Moreover, I can't drink because I will be driving. However, I shall certainly drop you there.

The taproom bar didn't give a very good vibe to me, especially looking at the exterior décor and the bass effects near the entrance. I felt it is certainly not a good choice to escape the rain and enter this space. But, by the time my mind can even figure out or debate, GP was already occupying a table. His shirt is tucked out from the tight belt, and even the second button from the top is released as if he is already basking in the flavor of freedom.

Why are you waiting at the entrance? You are not a security guard, step in fast.

Yes, this indeed looks awkward. I couldn't alter my shirt fittings, but, raised my sleeves partially, and pulled out the chair opposite to Guru, and sat down. As he was busy finding out all offers and bar menus, I was indeed taken away by the interior of the bar. It was so much having the feel of a well-known movie - The Good, The Bad, And The Ugly. And even though the music was Despacico, and people around were nodding their heads to its beats, my mind started playing the theme music of the movie. The wooden raw texture, the font, and the texts, the dress code, everything just coined together, and I could well imagine Clint Eastwood sitting on the opposite table by now.

Good Heavens !!! Did they get a Clint Eastwood in his 60's doppelganger? Who is that man?

An old man, wearing a hat, which is not the stereotypical cowboy one, but pretty much in resemblance, was the person I glanced upon. His thick glasses have the old brown frame which my grandmother also used to have at one point in time. The temple of the glasses is hooked to a leather neckband with fine needled artwork. The shirt collar was tied with buttons, and over to that, there was a thick metallic badge with fine carvings, which was hung as a necklace. Further to it, there was an apron which he wore, a velvet black textile, which indeed may sound like chef attire, but, here, it was more like a royal gesture. The full sleeve shirt ended with sharp shining cufflinks. The wrinkled skins of his hand were glorified by some gems across his fingers. This is even better than Mr. Eastwood.

As I was staring at the detailed attire, the old man noticed it, and as I looked up to his face again for a rescan, there was a subtle smile at one corner of his lips, just like Sylvester Stallone. He stared at me, and made a gesture with his eyes, offering me to take the empty chair to his table. I turned around and saw, in case that was a misjudged signal...

Yes, you... come and take a seat here.

Ok, that's a clear confirmation. Now Guru turns back too, and he was already enjoying the adrenaline rush with the happy hour offer.

Hi grandpa, good to see you here too...

Do you know him?

Of course not, but he is cool.

"Shut up. You order whatever you wish. Get me a sandwich, with extra cheese. I will be back.

And, I stood up on my feet, to drag it a few steps and sit with the old Cowboy.

I guess my attire has amazed you too much or is it like I am looking pretty funny?

Oh no Sir, actually....

CJ...Call me CJ

CJ? Like what's the full name?

Clinton John. My roots are in Mumbai. However, I was born and brought up in New Jersey. Now I have come back to spend the last innings of my life out here.

I see. So, what got you back to Mumbai? I am sure the quality of life in New Jersey would have been much better than here. This daily rush, Mumbai monsoon, poverty, population, do you find this comfortable at your age now?

See, my dear friend...

Neil. You may call me by this name.

Just Neil?

Indranil Mukherjee. So, friends call me...

So, IM, you see, it's not that you always have to have something good. Sometimes, even the worst will help you realize what good you could have done. It's a deep philosophy; you won't understand it without a sip of liquor. So, what's your poison?

I gave an absolute blank look to him, which made it evident that he read my mind.

... Ahhh, not a frequent drinker. That's why your friend got you here ....

I turned back and saw Guru holding the big beer mug with two hands and gulping it all. He just forgot that I was accompanying him. This suddenly made me realize, why was I here for? I looked outside to check the downpour.

Sit IM, we just met, and this rain will take another 30 minutes to calm down. A screwdriver is good for you? Or a mock-tail?

I have to ride my bike back home, so...

Waiter, get a Raspberry Mint Limeade, and a sandwich for this young gentleman.

What about you, sir? ...I mean, CJ.

Ahhh, they know me very well. They know what I want. I don't need to repeat my order.

So, don't you get bored having the same order every day?

CJ liked my question. He smiled and nodded with a mix of yes or no, which was very confusing to me.

Yes, sometimes I do get bored. That day I skip. But at this age, I don't try anything new, apart from the company. I get my flavor, not from the drink, but the company I choose. That friend of yours works in the same company you do?

Ya, we are colleagues.

But not friends I guess….

No, not like that. It's casual. He wanted to come here and was looking for a company. I had a choice to wait at the office till the shower reduces a bit, but.

But I hope you are not regretting the choice you took.

Of course not, it's a nice place, I liked the aesthetics and…

I was talking about the choice of leaving your casual friend at his table and joining me here.

Aaaa…Nah… not at all.

Ah, right you are. This sounds very odd to this entire décor. Any suggestions? I will improvise it.

You?

Ya, I am the owner. So, I will instruct the Manager.

I am sorry.

Why sorry? Rather I should thank you. I sit in this corner and I observe the crowd daily; how they enter, how they sit, their posture and reactions, how they behave.

Mostly I get to see people like your casual friend, engrossed in Happy Hours. But very few look around so critically particularly after the menu card is dropped at their table. They hardly even give much attention to my weird attire.Ok, may not be weird, but out of the box. You were out of the box too. And indeed, you have sharp observations, my young friend.

Thanks.

I am sure you must be hungry. Here comes your order, and my rum. Thanks, Martin. We'll ask if anything else is required.

So, what got you back in Mumbai?

Roots, my dear friend. I believe you are a Bengali and from Kolkata. Tell me, how do you like this city?

Nice, I love the fast life, the opportunities, the freedom.

You talk just like my father. He was just like you. He used to love New Jersey, the lifestyle, the freedom, the opportunities. He tried his best to sell this ancestral property and take my grandparents permanently with us. But my grandfather never agreed upon. The rat race is not just in Mumbai, it's everywhere. Maybe the pace differs, but, it's like, the grass on the other side is always green. We all got busy in our lives, and we hardly realized that slowly, we are getting engrossed in our requirements, and forgetting our roots. We didn't have mobile facilities in those days, but we had a landline. Still, we used to call our grandparents on Sundays. One such Sunday, the line didn't connect, and we poured the wine, thinking of some connection error. Later, we got to know that there was a major fire break out in our building, which had churned five families.

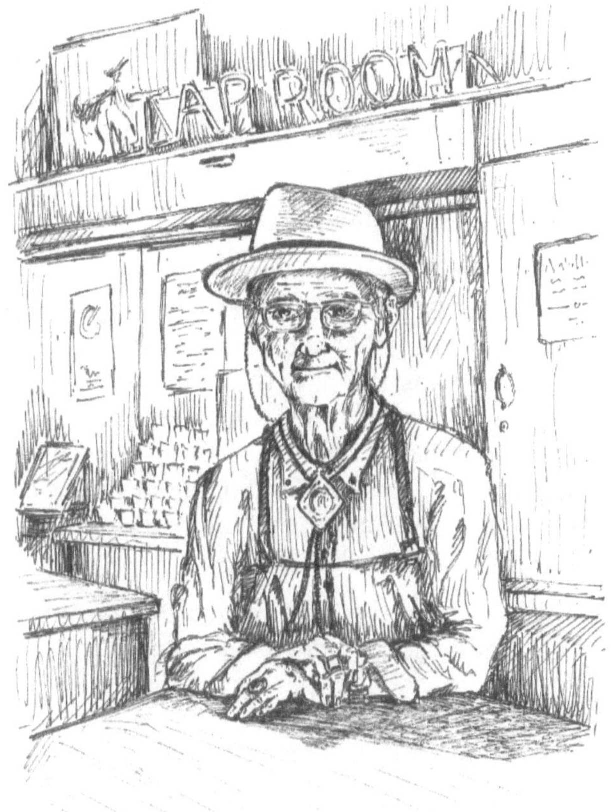

Oh… I am sorry to hear that.

Yes, that's how life is unpredictable.

So, then your family came here? For the ritual….

Yes, my father came alone. Foreign travel was not so affordable for our family, and this was unexpected. I was only 14 at that time, and I had my school exams. My father had bought this apron and this badge for my grandfather. He used to adore Clint Eastwood and make hairstyles just like his latest movies. For the rest of his life, my father always regretted that he couldn't gift this attire to my grandpa. And when he brought this for the final ritual, hardly there was a body to identify.

So, thereafter you all shifted here?

No, not so fast IM. You know money; doesn't allow a person to make easy choices. My father had nothing left in Mumbai, and he could not leave his job. So, he went back. But that was the day, I realized, you can't buy everything with money, though money is necessary to survive. So, I took an oath, that I will make a lot of money, and come back to Mumbai, set up a small bar in memory of my grandfather, and raise a toast with new Indian friends... Cheers !!!

Cheers CJ. That's great. So now you are wearing that dress your father bought for your grandpa.

You are a smart chap, indeed.

What about your family? I mean your wife, kids. Where are they?

I lost Mary a couple of years back. She was suffering and was bedridden for almost a decade. My son has settled in Singapore, he has a daughter too. Now, I have nothing else to take care of. But to live life wearing the shoes of my grandpa, and wearing the attire my father bought for him.

I am sure you are having the best days of your life.

Indeed I am. So, you see, sometimes, even the worse may open up your eyes to do good. That's why I am here, back to my roots. Enjoy the food.

CJ finishes his shot, pats my shoulder, and leaves the seat.

He is true, money-making does blind us. And I realized, it had been four consecutive days that I did not call my parents. But I am sitting in this Taproom with GP, who is now hugging me from the back for getting the entire bill redeemed.

And as the rain stopped, with the water cleaning the roads, it also gave clarity to my vision. The real value lies in the roots that we belong to. I took out the phone from my pocket.

Hello Maa, how are you doing? Is it raining in Kolkata?

Chapter 6

Desire Unfulfilled

Syed Saif Abbas Naqvi is a renowned philosopher and public speaker. He has quite a few books to his credit, where he has written about human rights and its misuses.

He was married to Nusrat and they had a daughter, whom they named Shabana. Shabana was just 2 years old when she had lost her mother, who died while delivering their second child, whom the doctors could not save either. The 2-year girl was thereafter taken good care of by Fathima, sister of Nusrat. When Shabana was around 3 years old, SaifSahab decided to tie the knot with Fathima. Within a year, Shabnam was born. In this family of four, the two half-sisters were just like best friends.

SaifSahab had his origin in Lucknow. His ancestors used to be the landowners there. But with time, the shine and pride of the family started fading slowly. It was SaifSahab's grandfather, who decided to start it all over again. So, he sold all his ancestral property in Lucknow and settled in Kolkata. He invested in textile trading and secured his family's future. SaifSahab's father was highly influenced by the cultural side of Kolkata. So, he never took interest in his father's business. He engaged his career in Literature, and so did SaifSahab.

However, the business is still managed by the family. Presently, Sulaiman Sheikh, cousin to Nusrat and Fathima, takes care of all the business. He has expanded the business from textile trading to costume designing. However, SaifSahab has not transferred the power of attorney to Sulaiman. All key decisions and financials are under SaifSahab's strict surveillance and control.

One fine evening after the college exams were over, Shabana had plans to meet her friends for a movie. She was getting ready to leave when Fathima arrived to play the spoil-sport.

Shabana, tonight we are expecting some special guests at our place. So, make sure you both sisters should be at home and do not plan elsewhere.

But Ammi, I already have plans for the evening. My friends will be waiting for me.

Who are they?

Rakhi, Meera, Rabia, Aakash, Nitin…

Ask the girls to come home tomorrow evening for your gossip, I will make special kheer for all of you. You know SaifSahab doesn't like you to mingle with boys. Let's not create any tension at home.

That's why I planned to meet them outside. They are my friends Ammi.

Ok, whatever, now get ready fast. No more argument, Text an excuse to your friends and make sure you wear the pink color salwar suit, that was stitched for the last Eid.

Oh my god, that's a gorgeous dress. Which special guests are visiting us that we need to deck up so loud?

Once they arrive, I will introduce them. Shabnam, you wear that light green one. Come on girls, get ready fast, and then help me out in the kitchen.

They both got ready as instructed by their Ammi and assisted her in the kitchen. As the doorbell rang, Fathima asked Shabana to wait there itself and took Shabnam along with. Shabana blindly followed the instructions. After some time, Fathima returns to the kitchen and asks Shabana to help her in carrying the tea tray. As soon as Shabana lifts the tray, Fathima pulls the veil from her shoulder and covers her face with it.

Ammi, what's wrong with you? Why are you hiding my face?

Just hold this tray properly. Make sure the tea doesn't spillover.

Ok, then remove the veil, I can hardly see through it.

Don't worry, I am holding you properly and guiding your steps. Make sure you don't remove the veil unless I ask to do so.

Fathima was so over-caring and conscious, which made Shabana worry a bit. She followed all instructions with no questions asked. She was guided to the center table of the drawing-room and was asked to place the tray on the table. Shabana tried to gaze through the veil and could see SaifSahab taking the single seat. Besides Shabnam, there were three more sitting on the couch.

By then, Fathima had left Shabnam alone and had taken a seat on the chair, beside SaifSahab. Soon, someone holds the left hand of Shabana and pulled her closer. Shabana was moving just like a puppet, with partial vision. That unknown grip loosened, and someone placed a ring in her fourth finger and kissed her left hand.

Subhanallah… Mubarak Ho…!!!… Everyone started wishing each other. Similar genders even raised from their seats and hugged each other, except Shabana. She still stood idle and without any reaction. She realized that she had just got engaged, and she could hardly accept that fact. She was shocked and silent and did not even remove the veil for the entire evening, till the guests left.

At night, she was in her room in a frozen state. Shabnam also sensed this tornado within her sister. She was also a bit numb. Fathima decided to break the ice and start a conversation.

Listen Shabana, you know how your Abbu is. Whatever decision he takes, it's only for the benefit and goodwill of you both, nothing else. This boy is a match in heaven for you.

Ammi what is his name?

Fathima, who started the conversation full of enthusiasm, was at a loss of words.

You don't even know his name. What does he do? Where is he from? Nothing. Ammi, you are my mother, I know Abbu loves both of us, and will never make a decision which will hurt us, but you… you are the mother too. So, don't you feel any responsibility as well?

I have faith in your father, and this was a very sudden decision…

How much sudden Ammi, that you didn't even bother to tell me? That means, you have the least concern for your daughter's future…Of course, I am your stepdaughter after all, why would you bother?

SaifSahab was overhearing the conversation from behind the door. He couldn't control further and decided to intrude in the discussion to conclude. He didn't enter the room but came close to the door and with his regular heavy voice, he made his point clear.

Shabana, behave yourself!!! His name is Naved … Naved Ali. I met him at the Hyderabad Literature Festival last year. I am confident, he is suitable for you. And you should accept the relationship. Now you both are engaged. We have fixed your marriage date too. Time is short, we need to arrange everything in 3 months.

But Abbu why so early?

It is not early, you are old enough to get married. One may consider the preparation time to be fast, but that's because Naved is shifting to Dubai in January, and both the families wish to complete the ritual before that. I have spoken to Sulaiman, he will get the fresh stocks by next week. Plan for your wedding shopping.

SaifSahab turned back and started walking to his room, and that was the end of the conversation. Like always, SaifSahab is a man of lesser words, but whatever he says, it is like a verdict, which cannot be altered. And now that the decision is reinforced, Fathima stood up to hug Shabana to console her hard acceptance. Shabnam too leaped from the bed to hug both tight.

That night, it was like a night without sleep for all the members of the family. No matter how rigid SaifSahab is from outside, but from deep within, even he was a bit upset that his daughter will leave the country soon. The stepmother's statement from Shabana troubled Fathima, made her feel guilty, for hiding this engagement plan from her. Shabnam was pondering what she should do in her life, after seeing the fate of her elder sister. She wondered why all this time Shabana had invested so much effort to fetch good marks in her academics, and what fortune is it going to bring to her now!!! She even thought of not continuing her studies further.

Shabana kept switching the table lamp on and off in a loop. Her mind was in serious turbulence, and her body was numb. The girl who was about to move out for a movie and spend the evening with her friends is now engaged to a completely unknown person, and she needs to plan for her wedding shopping. Life is so unpredictable, and democracy is so fake. She struggled to accept, but within a week, she was left with no other choice but to accept. She did not even have the urge to ask for a photograph of the groom to be. For her, if I am accepting what Abbu has decided, and I have no choice left, then what's the point? So, she decided to spend the last few days of bachelorhood with family in forged peace and started engaging herself for the wedding shopping.

Though it is the era of online shopping, however, SaifSahab trusts only Sulaiman, and none else. Sulaiman is a smart businessman. He involved his wife to communicate with the ladies and identify their choices. Shabnam and Shabana were enjoying their last few days together in that house before the marriage. Now that SaifSahab has given a free hand to shop for the occasion as well, they did not want to let this opportunity go. Both the sisters kept checking out all the wedding collections and photographs across social media and kept exchanging comments for them.

Shabnam, look at this photo of Virushka's marriage. My goodness, look at the lovely dress Anushka is wearing. I am sure this kind of dress will suit you very well.

Have you gone crazy? I am not any film actor. I don't even know how my would-be husband looks. And you expect me to wear this dress in my Nikah where I will have a naked waistline? Nice joke. These people can wear such clothes, not us. What's the use of watching all these? Ultimately, we are going to go to Sulaiman Mama, and he knows how to cover all the skin with thick textiles.

Let's share this image with Mami and tell her to convey it to Sulaiman Mama. At least let us try if he can create a prototype for you.

Do as you wish. We are going there today evening. Let's see what he has with him first.

As planned, the three ladies headed for Sulaiman's shop in the evening. They decided to take a metro and get down at Park Street. From there, the shop was a walking distance. Even though the destination was known, they enjoyed gazing across the big displays of the showrooms along the route and sharing light moments. All three were happy to exchange funny notes with one another. They took a left turn towards Kid Street. At that corner, there is a new showroom getting set up. It seems it is one of the renowned fashion designers setting up her boutique for traditional and bridal wear. Shabnam and Fathima were engaged in their conversation and walked past the window. Shabana took a silent halt.

She saw a person setting up a mannequin for the display. He dressed up the doll with an exotic saree which was making it look like a real-life diva. The person adjusts each fold of the dress with absolute care and pins them so that it doesn't get altered. Finally, when everything was set, the man switched on the spotlight and adjusted the light so that the rays lit the set up perfectly and the object of focus was the dress. The man moved on, but Shabana could not. She gazed at the mannequin, like she had been hypnotized and started conversing with it on her own.

You look so pretty and gorgeous. And even if you are facing the world, you don't have to hide with a veil. So lucky. I wish I could have this freedom to wear such lovely dresses as well. But then, society will start judging me. My parents will do it first. But you know what, I feel our lives are like the puppets in the hands of a male-dominated society at large. Even though I so much desire to ask this dress from you for wearing, I can't.

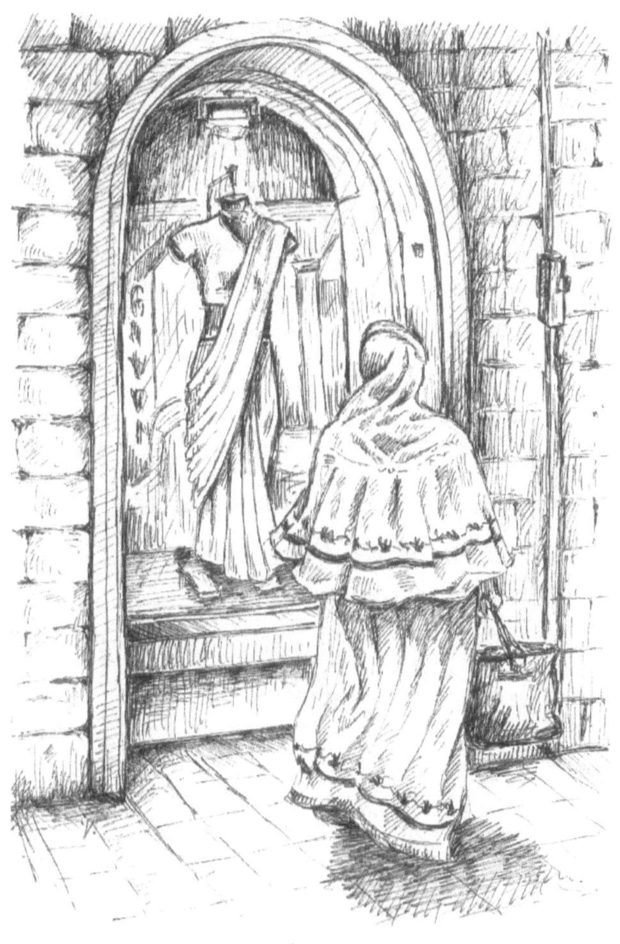

She was getting deep in her thoughts when suddenly a voice woke her up.

Shabana, why are you alone here? Fathima didn't come along with you?

Mami…how are you? Yes, they have just walked a few steps ahead. I guess by now they have entered Mama's shop.

Then what are you waiting for?

Nothing. I was just seeing this saree, isn't it so…

I know very erotic. I don't know how come they call this fashion. By the way, congratulations on getting engaged. SaifSahab was telling the boy is very handsome.

Yes, must be.

By the way, I was hearing SaifSahab's interview on the television that day. His speech was good and inspiring.

Yes, after all, the topic of discussion is best known to him… Democratic & Human Rights in Modern India.

Chapter 7

A Lie worth a Hundred Truth

101.2' - it's not improving as expected.

But Doctor Uncle, it's not deteriorating as well.

Dr. Pandey did not like the pointless optimism in young Devashish. He chuckled sarcastically and started packing his bags.

Do not give any more paracetamol to your father tonight. I have given him an injection, which will make him fall asleep soon. And this is a fresh prescription. Start these medicines from tomorrow morning.

Ok Doctor Uncle, please come, let me see you off till the main entrance.

The bedridden person is Digvijay Mishra. He had dedicated his life to the Bateshwar Hindu Temple in Madhya Pradesh, in India. He was a priest by profession, taking up the daily worship and rituals of the temple with utmost devotion and care. This fetched him deep respect and trust and he got so engrossed in this activity, that he did not marry. And he never repented for this. One fine morning, he found a new-born child left unclaimed at the footsteps of the temple. Digvijay looked around and even called others for any assistance. But finally, when he was convinced that the child was indeed abandoned, he decided to take him home. After a month's wait, when he did not receive any claim or inquiry for the missing child, he decided to name him Devashish and adopt him. That is how they both met and lived together thereafter.

Digvijay did not compromise on the child's upbringing. He gave him the education in the temple school, where he was introduced to Indian Shastras and Vedas. He also started involving Devashish in the temple activities, as he started growing up. As Digvijay started aging, he decided to voluntarily retire from his duties and settle down in his village. He insisted Devashish to stay in the temple and continue his studies and temple activities. However, the rich culture of the child did not allow him to shy away from his responsibility.

They both traveled back to Digvijay's small house in a village in Bhind district, of Chambal division in Madhya Pradesh. Though Digvijay did not wish Devashish to give a break in his studies, he indeed needed a companion to support. The small cottage was kept close for many years. They both somehow managed to restore the accommodation and set it up for survival.

Even though the house was far off from the temple where Digvijay used to work, his dedication and purity had earned him deep respect across his villagers. Hearing the news of his return, they made frequent visits to check if anything was needed. Devashish got admitted to the village school and he also continued his studies, though, in a different format and curriculum.

But within a few days of the relocation, Digvijay fell ill. Devashish tried with the ayurvedic medicines for a few days, but when it did not improve the situation, he was suggested to call for Dr. Pandey, who was the only allopathy medicine practitioner in the village. The young boy did not face such a hard situation in his life. Mentally, he was exhausted. So, right after the doctor left, he switched off the lantern and fell fast asleep.

The next day, Devashish woke up by his father's panic call.

Debu, wake up…!!!

Yes Bapu, are you okay?

I can't see things clearly. Something must have fallen in my eyes. Fetch me some water.

Yes, here you go.

Digvijay splashed water rapidly on his face and eyes, but the vision did not improve. Digvijay realized that there must be some serious issue that is barring the clarity in his vision. He did not intend to add tension to Devashish's young mind and pretend otherwise. But Debu got the hint of his overacting. He went out to consult the issue with the seniors in the village. The issue was a grave concern to all the villagers, especially when the same problem started troubling many others as well. The matter took no time to call for a meeting with the village Panchayet. The debate and discussion continued for a few days, at the end of which, the only common point observed was Dr. Pandey's injection. Without further investigation, villagers started avoiding the doctor's consultancy any further. But that did not provide a remedy to the already infected patients.

Digvijay had accepted the fact that his vision will never be clean anymore. With age, the opacity of his vision kept on increasing. With the loss of vision, his activities shrunk, giving him ample time to idle as well to reminiscence his past life. Every night after dinner, Debu used to see his father lying on the bed in absolute silence and nod his head slowly to himself. He had grown up by now to understand the indication, and he used to question Digvijay...

Now what?

What?

What are you thinking so much?

All my life I had served God and was always honest in my work. I am just thinking, what did I do wrong that I am cursed like this.

Bapu, it's an accident. Like you, many are suffering. Even Doctor Uncle left the village after people started avoiding him.

No Debu, always remember that karma always makes your payback.

But you were honest across your life, that's what you told me.

Yes, most of life…. When I was young, I lied to my best friend Ramlal. To date, I repent for that deed.

Come on Bapu, one lie cannot let you pay for your vision. God is not so unjust.

It was not just a lie. It was a cruel act. I was about ten years, when both my parents and Ramlal's, together, planned to visit Varanasi. Both of our families were very close. We used to go to the same teacher, and they used to stay in the hut where Manohar and his family stays now.

That's pretty close, about a hundred steps.

Yes. We were good friends, but Ramlal used to tease me in front of others for my short height. He was younger than me in age but had grown a few inches more at that time.

That's common, friends do make fun of each other. So, what happened at Varanasi?

We were playing in the water close to the footsteps. I thought, maybe that was my time to play a prank with Ramlal because I knew swimming, but he was yet to catch up. I showed him how to stay inside the water and travel like a submarine. With usual child instinct, he tried but didn't succeed. I enacted to teach him the trick, but intentionally turned him towards the stone pillar of the steps and pushed his body beneath the water level. The impact of the sharp edge on his eyebrows made him bleed in no time. Even I was afraid to see blood coming out. My parents came running to save him. They scolded me in public. I was afraid and lied that I didn't do anything. I pretended as if I didn't know anything, and that I was asking Ramlal not to try out such tricks.

And Ramlal Uncle also kept silent?

He was almost unconscious by that time, and he was rushed to the nearby ayurvedic center. He was hurt badly. But, later, he never opened up on this...

So, this was what you lied about?

It did not end there. You know what, after a few months Ramlal had to take specs to read books. The last time I met him, before leaving for Bateshwar Temple, he still had that scar on his eyebrows and a thick glass on his eyes.

Where is he now? You can say sorry to him.

No clue, where he has gone. But, karma, that never leaves you behind.

Yes, you are right, he used to bully you, so he got his karma balanced with those thick glasses and a scar.

And now, because I was involved in his compromised vision, the almighty is doing the same to me.

Seriously Bapu, you are taking your thoughts way beyond.

I am serious. That is why I always tell you, you should never tell a lie, no matter what the consequence is. I don't know how many years I have with me, but I just wish I can at least see the world clear one day before dying.

Bapu, please don't say such things. There is a new Vaid in our neighboring village. I have heard, he is just like a magician. We will go to him once to consult.

Already we have spent so much, but no result. No medicine will solve this.

Then what will?

The Ganges will.

What?

Yes Debu, the Ganges. The place where it all started. We need to go to Varanasi.

Bapu, look at your health. In this condition, how will you travel to Varanasi?

Don't worry. I will secure my last breath till I reach Varanasi.

But Bapu, already we are pushing the limits to fetch the basic daily meal. This travel cost will compel us to borrow money from the Munshi.

No ... no, I have some hidden treasure. Check the rice container in the kitchen, there I have kept some cash for an emergency.

And that's already consumed for the health emergency, the last time when you got senseless due to high fever.

And my piggy bank kept in front of Goddess Laxmi?

Your last year's wish to purchase a new bell for Yashoda, remember?

Who Yashoda?

Bapu, our cow. I wish to influence the grey cells in you, which can dig deep to 60 years behind, and makes you forget a year-old incident.

That is the indication. Debu, I don't want to listen to any more excuses. Arrange for my travel to Varanasi. I would like to go to the Ganges out there and take a dip. Everyone across the globe comes all the way to clean their sin in this holy river, and I have polluted that holy spirit by my insensible act and lying, that too standing over its footsteps. I will get no space in heaven after death, I must clean this sin before I die.

Poor Debu was in a dilemma. Now he started pondering to find the best possible means to connect the dots. One side, the finance, which was already in a bad shape. But much beyond that was his concern to make his 70 years old Bapu travel 500 kilometers. Like always, he started discussing the possible ways to implement the plan with his fellow villagers. Most of them made a clear point, that it will surely be a suicidal attempt. Many exploited the situation asking him to rent a motor van to plan the travel.

One fine morning, Debu woke up early and walked all the way to sit at the bank of a river in his village. He was wondering how to arrange for this wish of his father. He knew that his Bapu had done a lot for him, selflessly, even though he was abandoned by his parents. And that was the time that he should pay back to him. As the sun was about to rise, he noticed a set of people on the other side of the river, who had gathered there for a bath. They all gave a dip, and with folded hands, started chanting, by facing towards the east. That was when Debu got a hint of what he should do. He ran back home in fifteen minutes, and with the gasping breath, called out to his father.

Bapu...Wake up.

Debu...!!! What happened. I thought you left for school. Where were you?

Guess what Bapu. We are going to Varanasi.

Are we? Seriously?

Yes, indeed... We are.

But, where did you get the money?

I have not received it yet, but I will be getting it soon. There is temporary work in the neighboring village temple, and they will give some amount, which will suffice our travel for a day.

See, I told you, it's the cycle of Karma. God has made way for it.

Yes, we will plan the visit soon, maybe this Thursday itself.

But how are we going?

We will travel in a motor vehicle.

Motor Vehicle? That will be very expensive? How much is the temple offering you? Debu, are you lying to me? Don't do so if you are actually, you can already see what a lie has done to your father.

No Bapu, I have spoken to the person in the temple. They are traveling to Varanasi for some work, so they agreed to take us along with them. But, we cannot stay there for long.

Not required. I will just take a dip in the Ganges and back.

Devashish didn't waste much time to arrange. He rushed to Munshi, to seek his car for a day. He had to share the entire situation with him to convince him. Munshi was not known to have a soft heart, but here, he was touched by the dedication of Debu.

How much money will it cost Munshiji?

How much can you pay?

I don't have much with me, but I can promise to send pure drinking milk to your family for your children for the next 3 months.

When do you want it?

I would require the vehicle on Wednesday late at night.

You will travel at night? The roads are very unsafe.

No...no, we will pretend. The vehicle may just make a trip to the banyan tree from our house, and back to our place.

Ok, and then?

Then early morning to the riverbank.

The one which is towards the fort?

Exactly. That's the one. And right after that we will return and release your vehicle.

But that's so close by, why do you need a motor van? Whatever. Fine, start sending the milk from tomorrow. I will send the vehicle with my driver as you requested.

Thanks a lot.

The plan was all set. That night, Devashish gave some medicines to his father, which induces deep sleep in Digvijay. Right after dinner, the vehicle arrived at the doorstep. Digvijay was happy to step in the van and sit. Before the van could have even reached the banyan tree, he fell asleep. The vehicle returned to a safe locality, and Devashish made his father sleep inside the car, all night long. The next day, before sunrise, he drove to the river bank and woke his father from sleep.

Bapu, wake up, see what is in front of you.

Have we reached Varanasi?

Yes, can you hear the Ganges? Step out. The sun is also about to rise. Get ready.

Om
JabakusumSankasyangKashayapeyangMahadutyim...

Bapu, wait for the sun to rise. Keep your clothes inside the car. Hold my hands and come with me.

Yes ...yes. I just can't believe that I have seriously made this.

As Digvijay stepped down in his village river with his partial vision, the daily visitors and their chant drew an impression to him of the holy water of Ganges at Varanasi. He stepped inside the water and took some quick safe dips inside the water. Then with folded hands, he chanted some slokas, praying God to forgive him for all that he has done badly in life. Devashish could identify the tears rolling down his father's cheeks. Once all the chanting got over, Digvijay felt relaxed and content, which left him to chuckle and smile to himself.

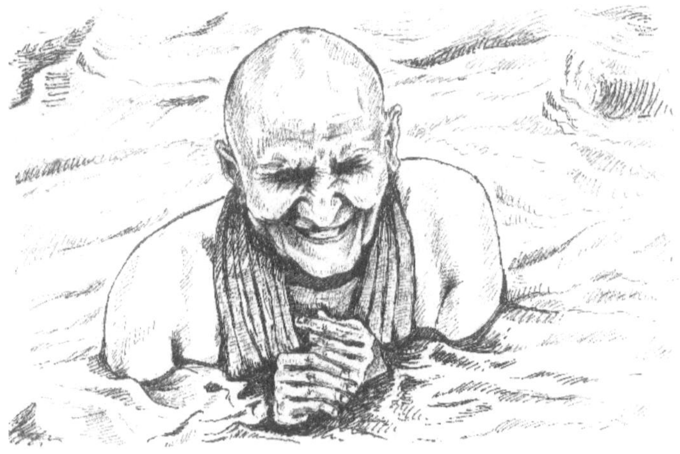

Enough Bapu, now you will catch a cold. Let's step out of the water now.

Debu, I can't explain how happy I feel today.

I can understand. Come, we must leave now.

Yes, let us move outside the water now. But Debu, I still cannot see things.

Don't worry Bapu, now that you have taken the dip, karma will favor you.

Yes, you are right. I don't know about myself; my days are almost over.   That you have made my wish come true, I bless you, your good karma will always be fruitful to you in your life. But remember, you should never lie in life. I don't want you to suffer like me.

Chapter 8

Happy Times Tough Times

It was an unusually silent morning in Haridwar. The chirping of birds echoed across the hills and magnified the eerie silence. The temple bells rang mostly due to the breeze and not through human connection. The holy Ganges kept on the barricading chain that was once meant for devotees. Everything was calm and quiet, as if, life had come to a halt. Beside the shops, many hermits used to rely on the offerings from the devotees and visitors. Things have become tough for them as well after this pandemic. Gyani Sadhu is one of them.

Raman alias Gyani Sadhu was brought up by Shambhu Baba in the interior parts of Uttarakhand. Shambhu Baba was a respected person, even by the neighboring villages. He earned his name for his in-depth knowledge and philosophies of life, which he used to relate with the mythological stories of Lord Shiva to preach to his disciples. Raman had always been highly influenced by those stories. But one day, a few villagers charged Baba with an allegation. However, considering the reputation of Baba, a few other villagers came to his support and brought the situation in control. Baba got extremely and the very next morning, he went missing. All his disciples looked around the neighboring villages but in vain. Depressed, even Raman left the village to travel across the pilgrimage sites of Uttarakhand to share those stories with people. Raman started leading his life on similar lines as his master, and this approach of Raman acquired him the name Gyani Sadhu. Many prominent groups of Hermits in Haridwar had offered him to join their gang, but Raman always stayed away from any attachment. That morning, Gyani Sadhu was sitting in a yogic pose under the shade of a banyan tree and was basking in the first rays of the sun.

The air was so fresh that Gyani could feel the supreme purity of nature. He was taking deep Pranayam breaths. But soon his meditation was distracted by a pungent odor. Such stinks are not unusual, but he looked around with the hope of having any human nearby, so that he may finally speak to someone after so many days. He noticed bare feet peeping from the tree trunk.

Hari Om...!!! Who is there behind the tree? Please come closer.

Gyani did not fetch any prompt response. After some time, he found someone trying to drag himself from behind the trunk and later crawled to reach close to Gyani. He seemed to be a Naga Sadhu, with a human body with no piece of cloth, and no bathing or hygiene for ages. His hair got tangled from the roots, just like the banyan tree. His skin was rough, with ashes and rashes across. His feet had a wound that was exposed to the flies to have a treat.

Sadhu baba, do you have some stock with you. Share with me then.

As he opened his mouth, Gyani noticed his remaining few brown-yellowish teeth, that too blackened at the roots. Gyani had always heard stories about Naga Sadhus from his master. He thought it was a good opportunity for him to engage in some conversation with this man.

What is your name?

Name? I don't have one. What is yours?

I am Gyani Sadhu.

Huh, as if you are "sarva-gyani". Then I am Parmathma. Now, do you have anything with you, or you are simply wasting my time.

You seem to be hungry. I have this apple with me if you wish to share a bite.

Oh, come on. I am a devotee of Lord Shiva. If I start the day with an apple, my Lord will be upset. Cannabis, please.

I disagree with the fact that this apple will upset Lord Shiva. I am sure, no such master will. But, since you mentioned, let me ask, whether you know how Lord Shiva and cannabis got related.

Yes, I know, but still, I would not mind listening from the Gyani Baba... Please, enlighten me.

Well, it so happened that when the ocean of milk was churned by Gods and the demons for acquiring the elixir of life, a drop of that fell on mount Madra. A plant sprouted out from that droplet. A drink was then prepared from those leaves and Lord Shiva admired that drink thereafter. That plant that sprouted out is said to be cannabis.

Okay, but I have a different story at my end. Due to an angry discourse with his family, Lord Shiva wandered into the woods. It was hot, and the sun drained a lot of his energy. Over to that, the internal family conflict had also drained the Lord, mentally. He got exhausted and decided to rest. He soon fell asleep under the shade of a leafy plant. When he woke up, his curiosity led him to sample the leaves of the plant. To his utmost surprise, he got instantly rejuvenated, and thereafter, that plant, Cannabis, became the favorite of Lord Shiva. And cannabis has been consistently doing this great job to all those who are in pain and distress. Now, do you have anything with you? I am getting restless.

Well, I am sorry my friend, I do not have any cannabis with me. That is why I offered this apple to you. But I must say, I am impressed with the story you shared.

Gyani Baba realized that the Naga was getting irritated and losing his cool. He tried to divert his attention with another story from his Lord Shiva encyclopedia.

Don't get so excited. Relax, if you raise your temper so high, then maybe Lord Shiva has to offer the moon to be placed on your head.

One more story? Seriously?

Not a story, but we all know. After consuming the Halahala from Samudra Manthan, Lord Shiva's body temperature started rising abnormally. So, to cool himself, he placed the moon on his head, as it is believed that the moon is cool in its full demeanor.

Again, a different angle of the same incident. That the moon is placed on Lord Shiva's head has a connection to Daksha Prajapati.

Oh, I didn't know this one. Daksha Prajapati was one of the sons of Lord Brahma.

Yes. He had 27 stars as his daughters, who were married to Moon. One of those 27 stars was Rohini. The moon always had a special attraction and feeling for Rohini, amongst all 27 star-wives. This partiality caused trouble within the family and soon Daksha Prajapati also got to know about the same. He then warned the Moon to treat all his wives equally, unless otherwise done, he will start losing his shine day by day. But the moon couldn't change himself. This curse made the moon lose the shine, and he had to take shelter in the ocean. But it disrupted the balance in nature. To bring back the balance, all deities approached Lord Shiva and requested him to do something. It is then when the moon took refuge in Shiva's matted hair. Lord Shiva succeeded in growing the size of the moon in 15 days, and then again waned for another 15 days. This kept repeating in a cycle. By this, the curse of Daksha Prajapati was also honored. That is why today we get to see a full moon and a new moon. Though science has a different logic altogether.

This is indeed fascinating.

What fascinating...? Look at the fate of the deities. The family life and its troubles have not spared them as well. Somehow, we have made a better choice. Else we would have one snake around the neck as well.

The snake across Lord Shiva's neck is related to Samudra Manthan again, with nothing to do with family affairs.

It seems you have done intense research only on Samudra Manthan and connect all life incidents of the Lord to just one sole activity. But you went wrong again my dear friend. The snakes that we find across Lord's neck are the ornaments that he had received during his marriage with Parvati. There were cobras with rubies on its head which served as lamps during night-time for the couple. Marriage was so well defined with this cobra across the groom's neck. Now, you say what happened at Samudra Manthan?

Well, during Samudra Manthan, Lord Shiva consumed the dangerous poison. In that ocean, few snakes also drank the same poison. This impressed Lord Shiva and hence he accepted Vasuki, the king of snakes. The snake encircled around Lord's neck and thereafter helped to keep the poison stationed at the throat of Lord Shiva.

Gyani, I bow to you. I wish everyone could have experienced the good aspects of life only and have never come across the darker side.

The activity of churning the ocean, the great Samudra Manthan act was itself a Great Conspiracy and was politically motivated. The Gods took the help of the Asuras with false hope of eternity and thereafter offered them nothing but disrespect. This disrespect and disgrace are continuing for ages. But, what everyone ignores, is the fact, to make Samudra Manthan work, even the Gods had to take the help of the Asuras, else, today your stories would have not taken shape.

Raman was silent. He did not argue. He could not contest.

What happened, Gyani? Why are you silent now? This is what the fact is. We all just look up to a situation as it is portrayed to us. We never flip the coin to check the story on the other side of it. Look at you and me. What difference do you think we both have?

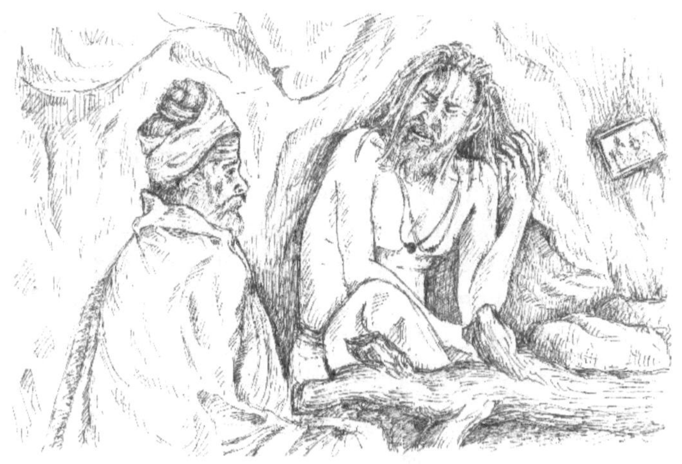

Wait… You and I have little in common.

Yes. We both are followers of the same Lord. But I have the image of the lord as a Tandava, you have his image as the Rescuer. You roam across places preaching his good stories and people offer you apples. I do the same, preaching the dark practical side of the same story, and they offer me bidis and cannabis. But, along with our approach towards the same Lord, our costumes are different as well.

Now that we both are sitting here under this tree shade on this lovely morning. In case if we could have had any devotee in front of us, he or she would have bowed to offer you a folded hand namaskar. On the other hand, I would have been highly ignored. In this same place, during the darkness of the night, I would have had absolute attention. Ultimately, we both are just like the two sides of the same coin. It's just like a back to back day and night.

Raman was left in deep thought by then. He could not argue with the strong logic that he confronted. And soon, he started believing in them as well. Slowly, he started admiring the stinking naked man sitting in front of him, with ashes across his body. He recollected how Lord Shiva appeared in front of Sage Parnada. He started having a feeling in his mind, as if, this Naga Sadhu may be a form of the Lord by himself.

My dear friend. I must admit, you have convinced me with your words. Indeed, life has two sides always, and it's always where we stand and which side we judge. But, rarely, I have ever seen a Naga like you with so enriched knowledge. Who was your Guru?

My Guru was a man of great honor and respect in our Naga community. Before joining us, he was one like you preaching the good to all villagers. He was very much respected, and people used to trust him a lot. A few key members of the local panchayat decided to exploit this trust and enforce some unscrupulous activity in the village, just for their gains. He denied the proposal. To retaliate, they alleged that he had molested a few women of the villages in the name of rituals. The villagers became furious and were almost on the verge of killing him. The very next day, he left the village silently and walked across the hills. He starved for days during this travel and was extremely feeble when we found him lying unconscious beside a cliff. We treated him for months and got him back to life. By then, he was one among us. Soon after, he started sharing stories of the Lord to us, and we started admiring him as our Guru.

Raman was connecting the dots by now, and every time things matched, his anxiousness increased exponentially. Before he could ask anything more, he connected the last dot. The Naga hits the final shot...

He was renowned in that village by the name of Shambhu Baba, but for us, he is Guru Rudra.

Is he still alive? Can you take me to him, please?

I guess he is, no clue. It's been almost a year since we met last.

Raman paused to bask in the naked truth of life and its changing colors. He then keeps the apple back in his side bag and reaches out to the side pocket of his gown. Takes out a bidi and lights it up. Takes few puffs, and releases the smoke in that fresh morning air, and extends the same cigarette to Parmathma.

Jai Shiv Shambhu...!!!

Chapter 9

Dilapidated

Show what you have got.

Yes, sure. I loved the way you smiled at the lens; it gave a lovely candid moment.

Take one more, I am holding the newspaper as if I am reading it.

Yes sure...!!!

Anirban Koley, a working IT professional from Bengaluru was in North Kolkata that Sunday morning. He was there with his brand new DSLR. His parents were permanent residents of Bhawanipur, from South and relatively modern Kolkata. This year Anirban was fortunate to come home a fortnight before his planned schedule, thanks to his urgent office project. And that was the time when the city was getting ready for the upcoming grand occasion.

Kolkata is the cultural capital of India, for its rich literature, art, drama, cinema, intellectual thoughts, and contributions from many dignitaries across several fields of activity. The city also has tremendous historical and architectural significance. Kolkata has evolved with time in terms of lifestyle, just like other metros. However, the northern part of the city still has most of the old buildings standing strong. While the world is in its concept of constructing a residential society with tall towers having several flats and studio apartments within, this old architecture promotes space and perfect air circulation. Many have the projected veranda for a perfect panoramic view, and the open space to sit and gossip. That, this area still brings back the nostalgia, has become the photographers' paradise.

Anirban also could not resist capturing this charm through photography. In his expedition across the by lanes of North Kolkata, he started clicking an old man sitting on one such roadside open platform of the house. The exchange of words slowly shifted from photography to personal.

So where do you stay son?

I work in Bengaluru. Here my house is at Bhawanipur.

You have come at the perfect time of the year. Durga Puja is just a few days away. I hope you will have quality time with your parents here.

Yes, of course.

Durga Puja is probably one of the biggest festivals of India and beyond, where Art Installations creates a new benchmark. The citizens anxiously wait for this time of the year. Almost all who have their families and relatives or any connection with the city, try to attend this great cultural festival. As you know, the entire city has innumerable 'pandals' all across. But besides that, many families perform their family rituals, which are being continued as a tradition for ages.

Anirban was curious to observe a few of such private traditional worships that year.

Uncle, I have heard this north Kolkata area has many more traditional Family Durga Pujas, besides the renowned Rajbaris.

Yes, you have heard it right my son.

Do you know any such house nearby? I am curious to see how they have started taking their preparation for the festival.

The old man folded back his newspaper and kept it beside him. He gestured Anirban to take a seat beside him and ordered for tea.

Bishu … two numbers of special tea … served in earthen pots.

How do the earthen pots make tea special?

Well, for us it's nostalgia. But in true essence, it's the earthen touch. Sip to understand.

Yes, the tea tastes refreshing.

The same is with the lesser-known family Durga Pujas, just like this tea.

Sorry uncle, I didn't get you.

You get tea mostly in your favorite Cafeteria in the shopping mall, and you pay a hefty amount for it. You even put up social media posts for checking in to that place. Don't you?

Yes uncle, we often do so.

But will you ever put a social media post for having this refreshing cup of tea at Bishu's Joint? I understand you may be trolled badly thereafter.

Anirban was silent. He agreed that people often tend to ignore what is available, easily or freely or locally.

Kolkata Durga Puja is also just the same. People flock only for the renowned clubs, where there are huge banners, themes, grandeur, and of course loads of advertisement. They stand in a queue for hours, push each other, and toil to get a glimpse of the artwork. I am glad someone from the present generation has some inquisitiveness about the not so advertised family rituals, as well.

Go straight this side, leave out the first, and take the second right turn. You will find a sweet shop on your left side. Just the third building from that sweet shop is one such destination. It's the Das Family.

Oh, thanks a lot. Will they allow me inside? I am a stranger.

Give it a try, you have nothing to lose. I hope they won't mind.

Thanks, uncle.

My pleasure. But just one thing, don't expect much. I don't know whether this year they are even doing the ritual or not.

Anirban quickly finished his tea and started walking towards Das's mansion. As he stepped closer, he started imagining the surprise element. But the last statement of the old man rang in-ears too. The conflict of hope and despair could not lead to any conclusion.

Soon Anirban stood at the main entrance of the house.

The main door was elevated from the road level by three concrete steps, supported by heavy circular columns. Anirban stepped forward to knock on the worn-out wooden door with a heavy door handle. In his attempt, the right half of the door got enough thrust to open up partially. He peeped through the small slit of the two doors to check out the partial view of the interior. An open big space, veranda, and circular decorated columns to the left side and is expected to have a mirror image to the right side as well. Anirban shouted out loud through the door gap ...

Hello...Anyone there?

His question was promptly replied to by a few pigeons who made random flights inside the house close to the door shed. But no human intervention or response. Anirban tried to safeguard himself from any charge of trespassing and did not make any attempt to step inside. He slowly opened the right pane of the door wide and bent forward to call out for some assistance.

Hello...Is there anyone in this house?

This time, even the pigeons did not react. The interior was now clearly visible to Anirban, and he could notice a partial ready idol across the open space. Seeing that, he took a breath of relief dismissing the old uncle's doubt. At least, this year the Puja is still in place. And by seeing that, he also gathered the confidence to step inside the house.

Anirban took cautious small steps as he headed straight towards the idol framework. The house seemed deserted, and his eyes kept moving in all directions to find at least one human intervention. Finally, he heard someone coughing from behind the pillars. He further headed straight and raised his voice for assistance. But no response yet. He was already in the middle of the open space. He took some confident steps to reach out to the source of the coughing sound.

Behind the pillar, he found an old man, much older than the previous one. Clad in an absolute milk-white traditional kurta and dhoti, this old man was sitting on the floor, and cleaning the weapons of the Goddess. Anirban presumed that due to age and associated hearing problem, he may not have heard him from outside. This time it worked.

Yes, who are you?

I am Anirban. I am...

Who? Nipen? Whom do you want to meet?

No, no Dadu, Anirban...Anirban Koley.

Ripon? Do I know you?

Anirban's top voice in that proximity was also in vain, and with every repeated attempt, he realized the old man was getting restless for the fact that he had a hearing issue. And just at that moment, a servant came running downstairs.

Dadu, plug in your machine. You both are shouting on top of your voice to the extent that it disturbed my sleep. Yes, Sir, who are you? What do you want here? And how come you enter our house without permission?

Dada, actually I didn't mean to trespass. I knocked on the door several times and then called out too, but didn't get any response…

Does that mean you will step in just like that? Now get lost. We don't have time…

By now the old man was ready with his hearing aid. Seeing the servant shouting at Anirban, the owner took charge.

Hari… Behave yourself. Enough is enough. How many times have I told you, not to be impolite to any guest?

But Sir … this young fellow has stepped inside without permission.

Yes, and I am the owner. I allow him. You may go now at… Yes, young man, Mr. NipanDholey.

Anirban Koley… I was informed by an uncle across the lane that this house hosts a family Durga Puja. I was out this morning to click some frames from North Kolkata, so thought to try out my luck.

I see. So Mr. Koley, welcome to Das Mansion. I apologize for missing out on your calls and also the trouble you had to face on account of this. I am Naba

Chandra Das, the descendant of Krishna Chandra Das, who started this Puja in the year 1826.

My goodness !!! Close to 200 years…

194…to be precise.

This is a heritage then.

Ahhh… I wish. But you know, everything doesn't fetch its deserving value. Sometimes, priorities change. Well, tell me about yourself. Are you a professional photographer?

No… no, Sir, it's just out of my passion. I work in Bengaluru.

Oh, lucky you! You got to come to Kolkata during the Puja. At one point in time, this house used to be filled up with people during this occasion. All family members used to gather, and many eminent personalities as well.

Are they not coming this year?

No Anirban, not just this year, it has been more than a decade that the Das Mansion Durga Puja has lost its charm along with the footfall, even for the family members.

How can everyone be so indifferent?

It's not just indifference; but, as I said earlier, priorities change with time. You tell me, why do you work in Bengaluru and not in this city itself?

I got a better opportunity there, so I decided to leave.

Exactly, that's what it is like. See, you prioritized. It's common and obvious and nothing wrong with it. The same is with our family. I am the youngest son, with 2 elder brothers and 1 younger sister. All brothers and sisters, along with their sons and daughters are settled abroad. All are busy with their work, their life, their priorities.

And your wife and children?

Well, my wife died about ten years back. She was suffering from cancer. I did my best but I could not save her. It drained most of this mansion's antique collection.

Oh, I am sorry to hear so.

I have one daughter, who is married and settled in Mumbai. I have a grandson too, very naughty. They used to visit us every Durga Puja, but for the past few years, my grandson's exams are getting scheduled during this time, which has spoiled my plans to meet them in person.

So, now in this huge house...

Just me, and Hari were there. Hari got married last year. So now his wife has also moved in here.

I see. Please don't mind, if I ask you something.

Please, young man, feel free.

I keep reading about the losing glory of royal and illustrious families, whether in Bengal or other states. The main reasons are financial issues and family disputes. Did the same happen to this family as well, because of which, this year, people doubted the Puja being conducted here?

Huh…!!! Really? People are thinking so? Till that I am alive, I won't let this Puja stop. A financial dispute within the family, indeed, to some extent has happened. It's no more like the good old days. Here, right in this place, there used to be a fine glass chandelier hung from the ceiling, which got sold to an antique collector. Inside in the drawing-room, a pure teak wood dining table for 12 seating, even a handwritten letter of Netaji Subhash Chandra Bose, and many such valuables I was compelled to sell one by one, that too for a failed bargain.

But you said your family members are all settled abroad. That doesn't give a hint of such a financial dispute.

Yes, we all think, money earned in dollars makes us rich. They all are wealthy indeed, but they have greed as well. Promoters are offering a huge sum for this entire space. All my siblings or their descendants are in favor of the offer. But not me.

Oh my God! Is that why they have stopped coming for the Puja as well?

Maybe. I think so. They have forced me many times to sign the papers, which I will never. Now that I have aged, all the promoters are anxiously waiting for my last breath, so that they get a clearance without any hazard.

Dadu, I am sure, if I would have been in your place, I would have given up.

It all depends upon the perspective from where you see things. One may see it as if I am going against my family. But I am safe-guarding my family tradition and culture to the best of my abilities.

Indeed, that's true. But hats off to your will power. It's rare to see someone like that.

Young man, do you see that huge bronze bell hanging? I remember, since childhood, I was given the responsibility of ringing that bell whenever the worship rituals were conducted in this house. Whenever that rings, I feel my youth. Many have offered me a hefty price for this one. Every time I sold something from this house out of extreme necessity, it has hurt me from deep within. But this bell is my source of motivation. Won't you like to take a few of my photos?

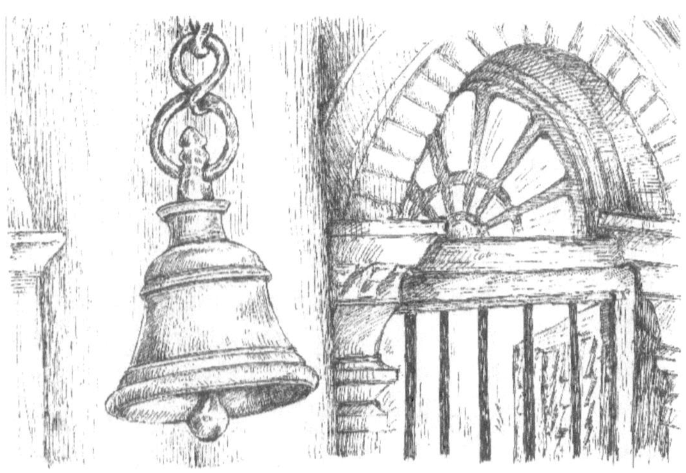

Oh yes Dadu, I was about to ask for that.

Saying that Mr. Das got back to his activity of cleaning the artificial weapons for the idol. Anirban took some clicks of him. With the weapons in hand, that old man appeared like a true warrior to Anirban. And just like the fairy tales, this soldier king had his life secured in the bell, the big bronze bell. Anirban took a close look. "Das Family" in Bengali font was inscribed on the bell. Anirban could not resist but to ring it once. The ring was sonorous. The inspiration of purity echoed all around.

So, Anirban, I hope to see you attending our family Puja. Whenever you are around, even with your friends, do drop in.

Sure Dadu. I promise I will.

And while you are leaving today, you will find Bishu, the tea seller.

Yes... yes, I met him this morning.

Yes, he will be waiting for you. Inform him, that this year, the Puja is happening here.

Anirban was surprised. The old man chuckled and further added...

That old man you met is one of the prospective promoters. Bishu is his informer.

Chapter 10

The Helpless Smile

Axon Pvt. Ltd had planned to construct a smart HIG housing society along the mountainous stretch behind Gachibowli in Hyderabad. The project was sanctioned by the government, and they have even commenced pre-bookings. "Parvaat Ville" was certainly one of the most overhyped projects in recent times. And to accelerate the work and complete the difficult target before monsoon, an excess number of laborers were deputed. Work had been progressing at its required speed, and everyone was happy for the promised payments reaching out to them.

But, the smooth workflow had a tremendous jolt with the onslaught of the pandemic. Taking into consideration the safety norms, the Telangana government made it mandatory for all developers including Axon to make sure that there should not be any work at the site till further notice. The entire site activity came to a grinding halt. The labor group leaders were informed, but there was much agitation amongst the laborers. So, to bring things under control, Mr. Mahendrakar, Deputy General Manager of the site, asked the labor group leaders to call all the members for a common discussion and announcement.

Mr. Mahendrakar was known for his rude behavior, which was always in favor of the company, no matter how hard it could strike upon other stakeholders. The labor group leaders were not keeping much hope from this meeting.

Tuesday morning, March 31st, everyone gathered in front of the small hillock on the eastern side of the site, near the water reservoir. All the laborers were waiting for Mr. Mahendrakar to arrive. With every second that passed, their heartbeats increased. Finally, the monotony of prolonged silence was crushed by the sound from a speeding vehicle. Everyone turned round to identify the swirl of dust approaching them. The laborers gulped the last portion of saliva and stood up on their feet with folded hands.

The maroon Honda city gushed through a gap between the laborers and stopped at the feet of the small hillock. After the dust from the surrounding settled, the door opened up. The thoroughly polished caterpillar shoes stepped out from the left. Mr. Mahendrakar adjusts his shades first and then his facial mask. The driver rushes to him with a huge umbrella and a portable microphone.

Mr. Mahendrakar nods a formal response to the folded hands and morning wishes from the laborers. He slowly moved towards the nearest high rise platform of the hillock, to justify his position and authority.

Dear all, we are now in a very difficult situation. As you all know, the government has asked for a complete lockdown across India. So, we doubt when we can resume the site work again. It's just a precautionary measure for you all. So, we request you all to stay at the labor camp itself and stay safe.

But sir, what about our food? We are daily laborers, if the work is stopped, how will it be possible for us to feed ourselves for all this time?

How may I comment on that? Ask your group leader. Santosh, Murli, Sudhakar, and whoever else, please look into the issue. The company is already doing the best possible. You have a secured shelter at least to stay. We are not asking for any rent. Be grateful to Axon, stay loyal.

Sir, we have served your company with utmost loyalty, working in this hilly terrain, breaking rocks, day and night, mostly over time, as and when you asked for it. Now…

Loyalty is expected, else why will the company retain you. You have done no favor, please understand that. And you have fetched extra payment for that overtime, so there is nothing to exaggerate about. Everyone has to manage the situation. Even we are doing.

But Sir …

That's all I have to say. In case if you wish, you may stay, else, proceed to your hometown. All the best.

Saying that Mr. Mahendrakar started trekking down the hillock, murmuring to himself.

The laborers were lost, looking at each other's faces and confused about what to do. The group leaders also had no way out.

The panic situation soon started getting worse and in such a tense moment, Sushil took the role of a responsible torchbearer, to lighten the moods.

Brothers, don't worry, this is India, and no one can sit idle for long. Things will settle in a few days, don't panic. Now just think to this point that tomorrow we don't have work to do. And I have a small portion of local liquor. So, who wants to see stars with open eyes?

Sushil, it's a national lockdown. Not a matter to take it so lightly.

So Mr. GajodharKanui, what do you suggest? Let's mourn this fact and sit idle?

And that soon erupted a sense of debate and arguments among the entire gang. No one had any specific answer and not much money as well. They planned to stock some grains for the next few days and see how things run till then. For the time being, they all decided to stay back at the labor camp, being afraid of the police patrols who could harass them on the streets.

But this situation extended beyond the timeline they expected it to be. All optimism slowly evaporated, and they could sense the grave situation they are in. By that time all commuting was also restricted by the government, as a result of which, the panic grew three-folds.

With no other option left, the laborers decide to pack their bags and start moving towards their village. What if they don't have trains and buses, they have their strength to walk the maximum way possible, and whenever they will fetch any commute, they will avail it for the partial travel. With this common confidence, everyone started packing up. Finally, with all the willpower, they stepped out on the roads for an infinite journey ahead of them.

As they started, there was fear coming out in the form of sweat from their wrinkled foreheads. The absolute deserted streets and the absence of traffic catastrophe - this was never even imagined, and that magnified their concern and fear even further. But, now there is no looking back. They have already overlooked the final warning of Mr. Mahendrakar, now, they don't even have the free shed of the labor camp. They all took a deep breath in the name of respective gods and agreed to accept the way it comes.

Gajodhar was leading the queue. He was just like another laborer and didn't yet prove to have an extraordinary skill set in his work field. However, he has this intense sense of responsibility towards his blood relations, as well as extended family members of the labor gang. People trusted him, and everyone agreed to follow a queue and move on.

Being in the frontline, Gajodhar was the first one to visualize this new world. The first sweat of fear was from his body for certain. But, he was a true leader and made sure that the panic doesn't get into the mind and soul of his group.

As Gajodhar was questioning himself and God almighty, about this extreme situation, he sensed a soft touch pulling his left-hand fingers. He looked down and saw his 4-year-old son Virender, pulling his hand and smiling.

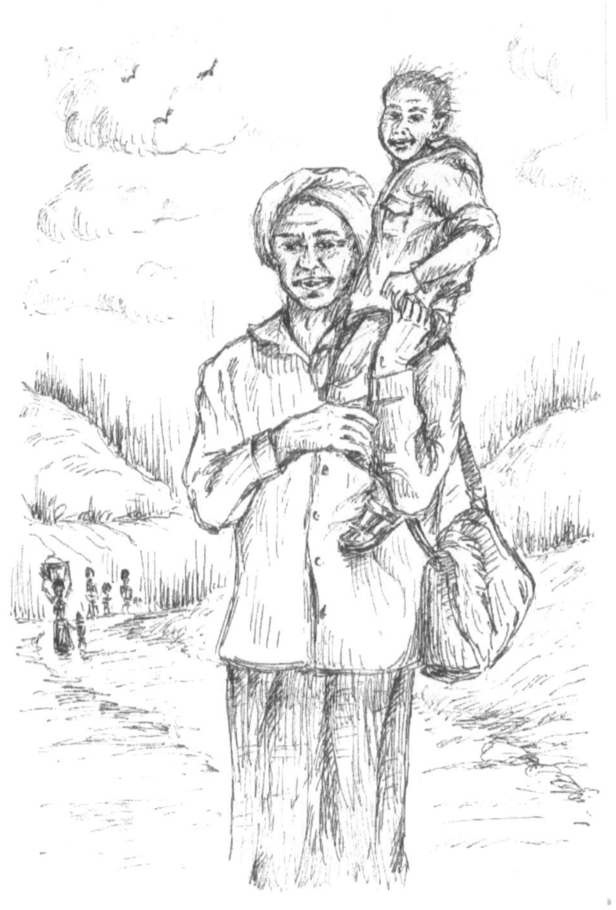

This sight of his smiling countenance melted away the panic. Gajodhar then stepped into the boots of Virender and tried to look into the situation from the child's perspective. Gajodhar realized that the kid finds this as a group tour, and he is happy that all are going together somewhere. For him, nothing is wrong yet, and he is basking in the flavor of the present. Gajodhar smiled back at his son.

The situation has not changed, nor the people and time. It's just the way of looking into things. Neither Gajodhar nor anyone else knows how far, how much, how long they will be able to make it. But it's today, it's now, which all make things happen. Gajodhar had a deep breath, to embrace this realization which made him feel confident, and stronger enough than before.

He felt the pull in his left hand once again. Gajodhar now holds the hands of Virendar tight enough in response to the pull, and the kid exclaimed in ecstasy. He lifted his son in his arms, and then further on his left shoulder, adding some careful tickling on Virender's belly. The expression of this wonderful bond between father and son filled the ambiance and echoed in the silent streets. It reached out to the others. Someone even suggested tickling him further. Soon, there was a light moment created.

Everyone felt energetic, and moved on with positive vibes, and smiles on their faces. Virender laughed louder and seemed to enjoy the ride.

Gajodhar kept the smile alive, even though at the back of his mind, he still had fear factors playing hard. And he continued to walk on... aspiring to find a solution to his existence in the name of god.

THE

SKETCHES

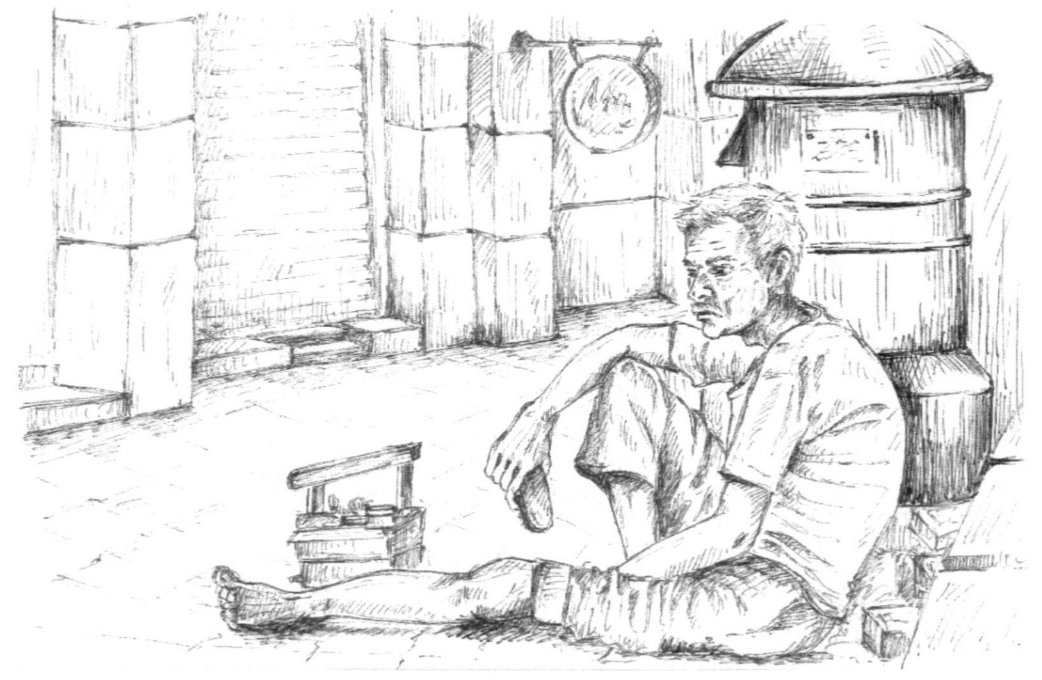

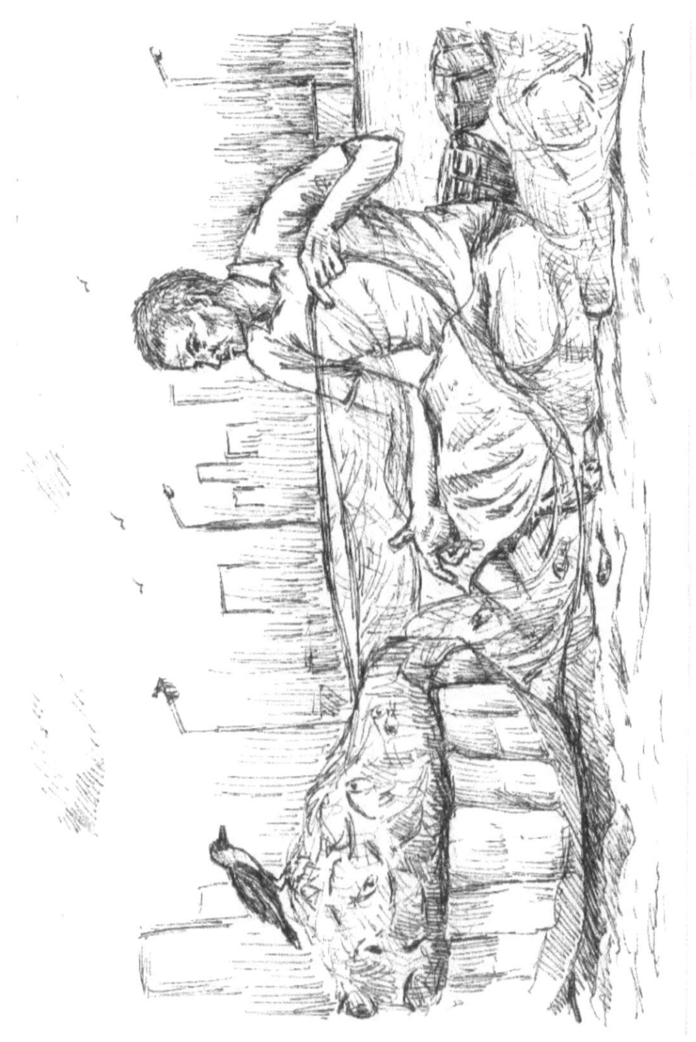

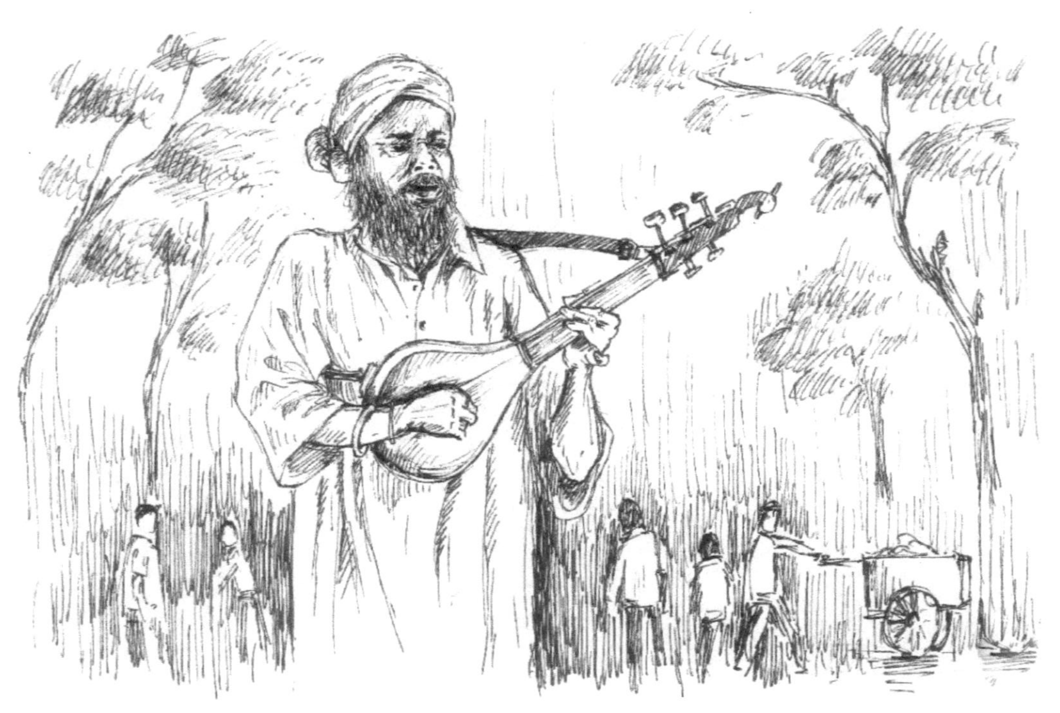

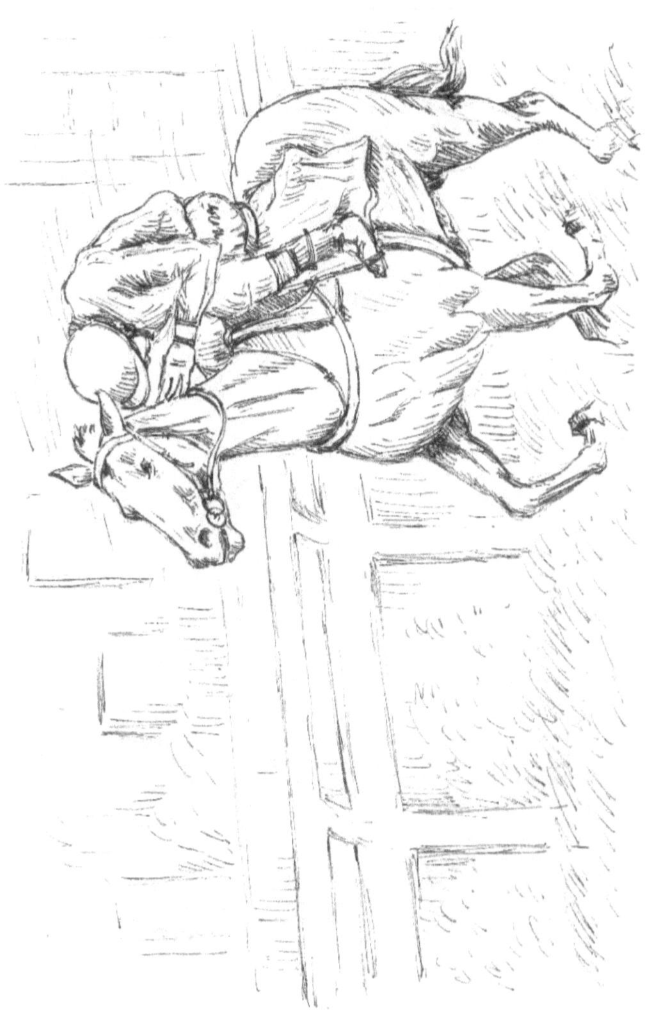

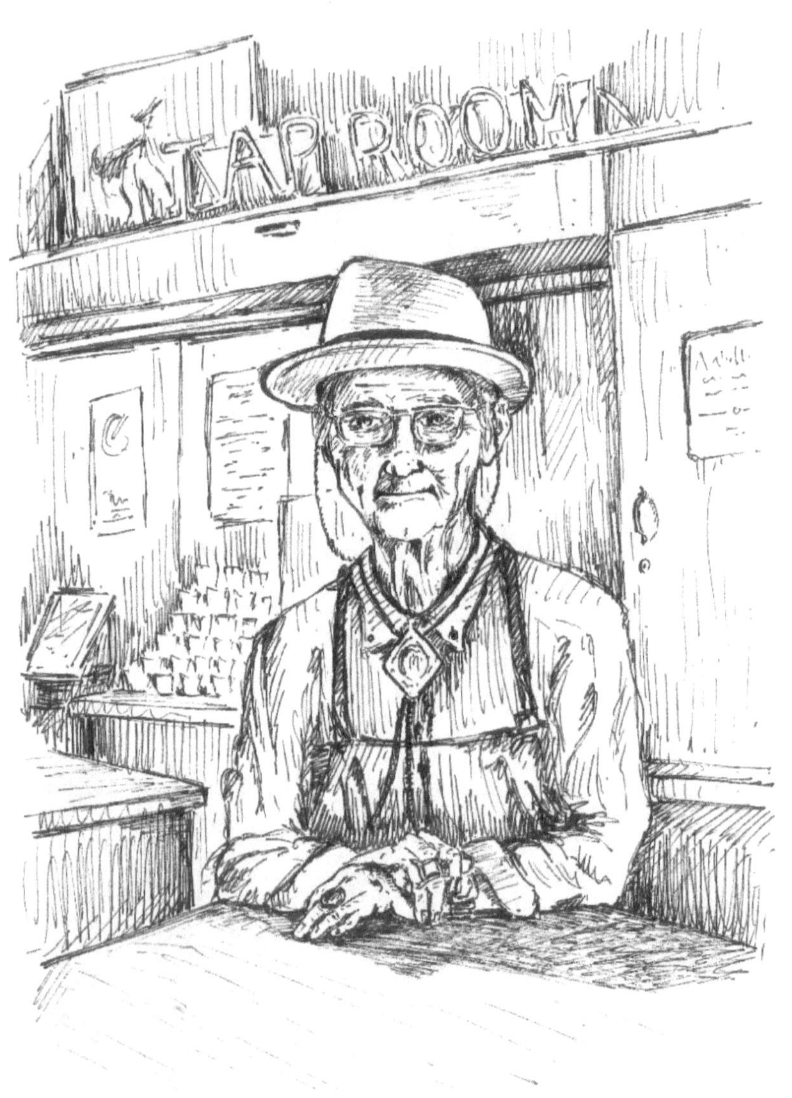

TAP ROOM

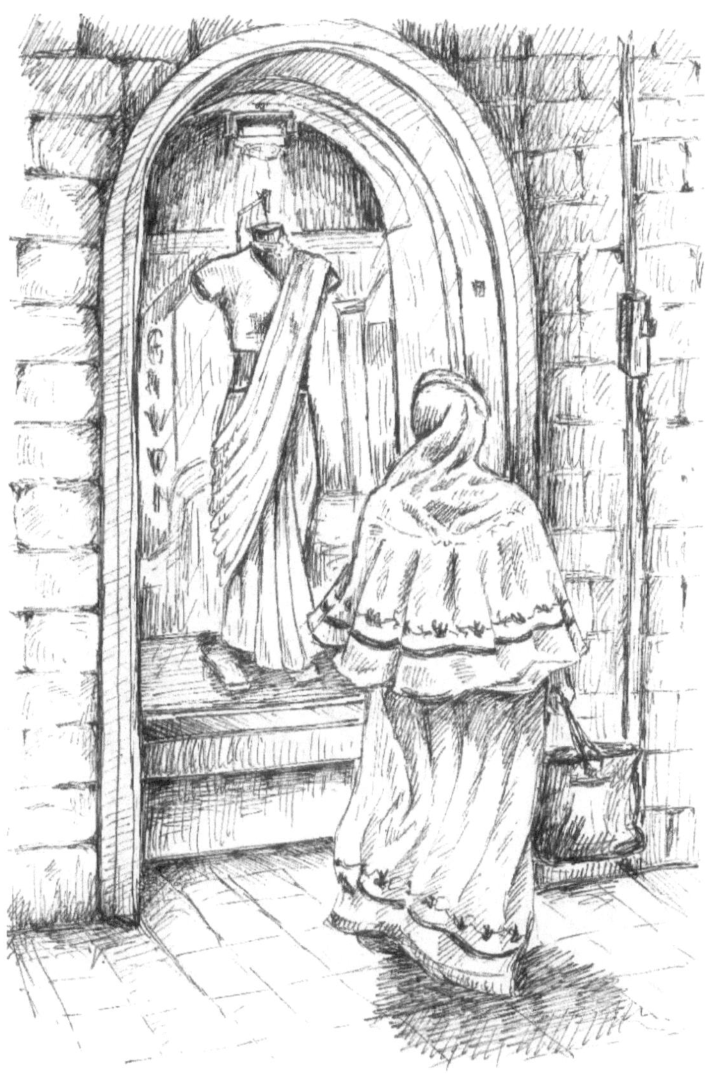

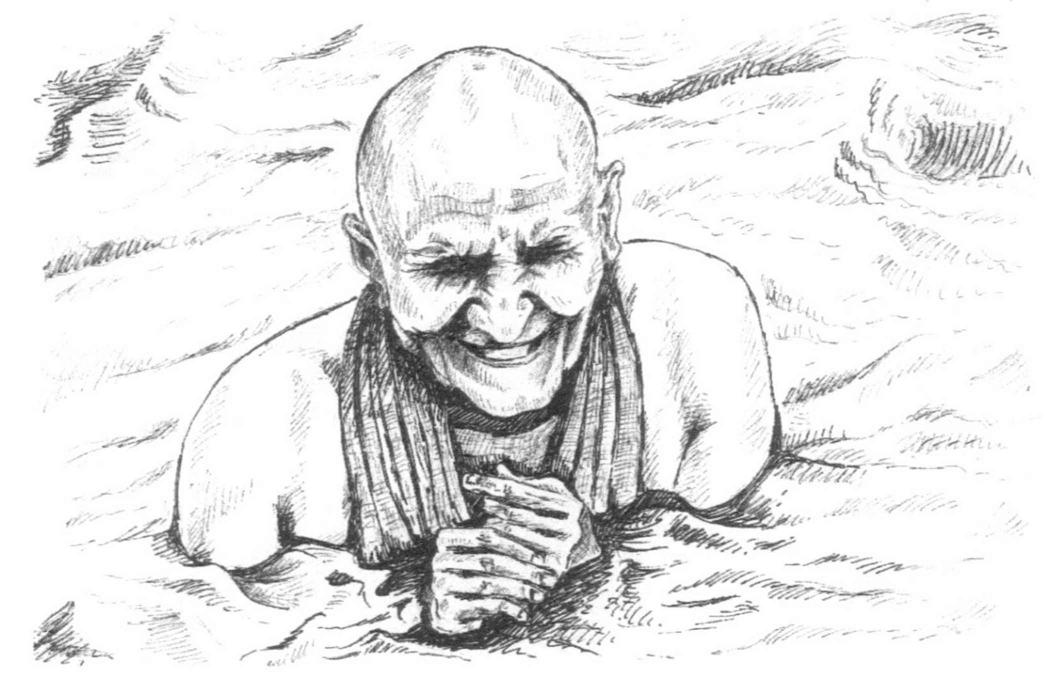

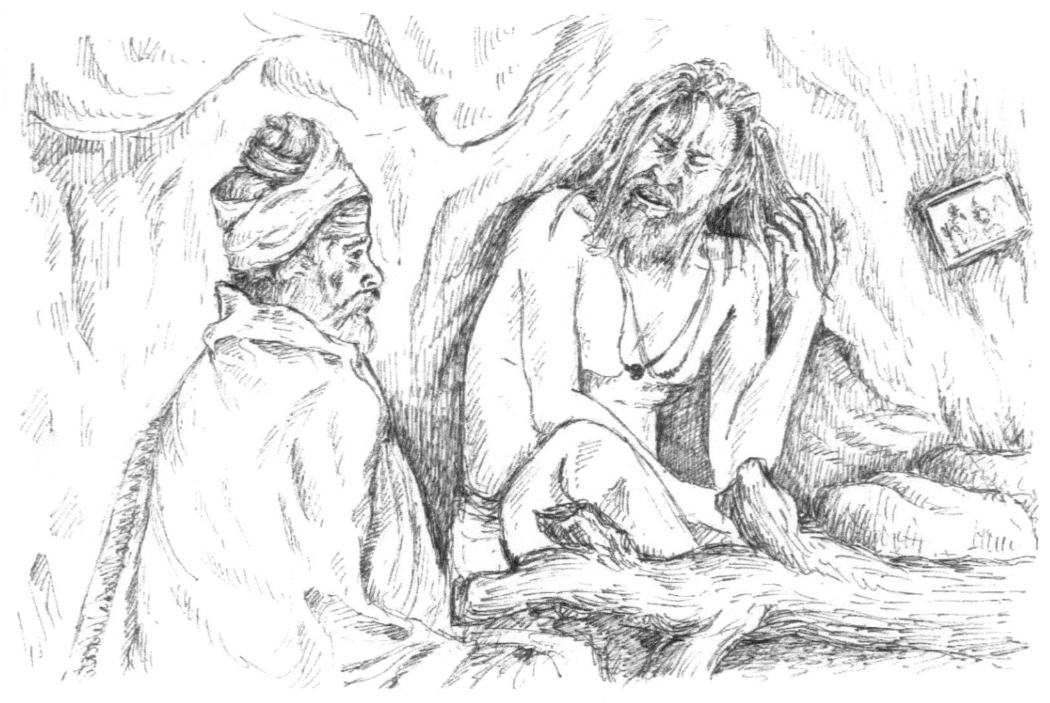

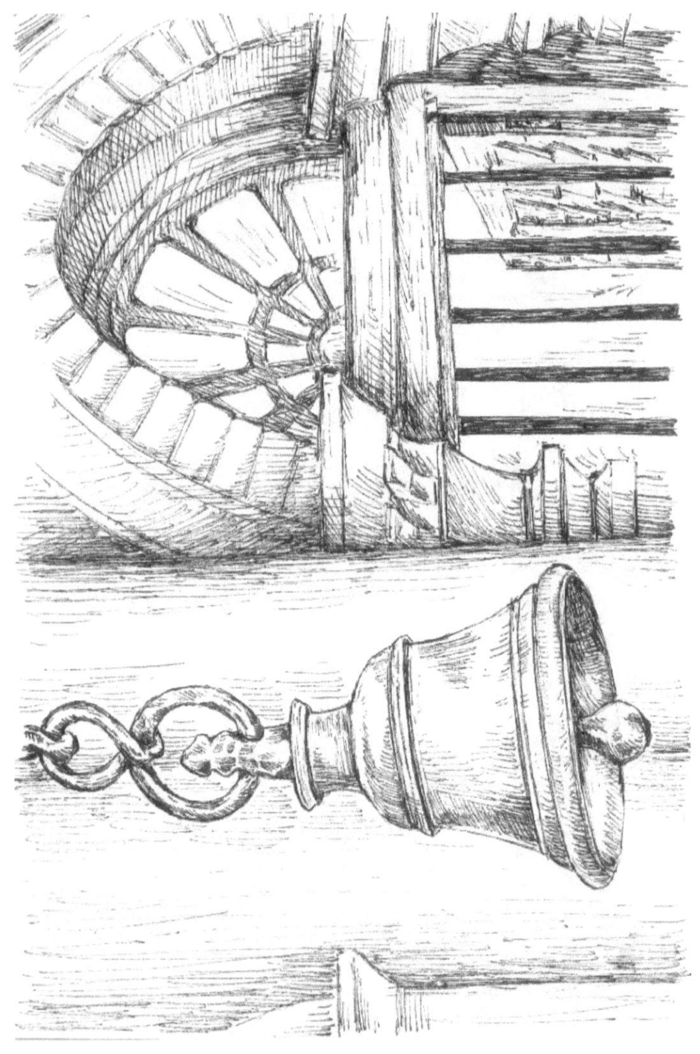

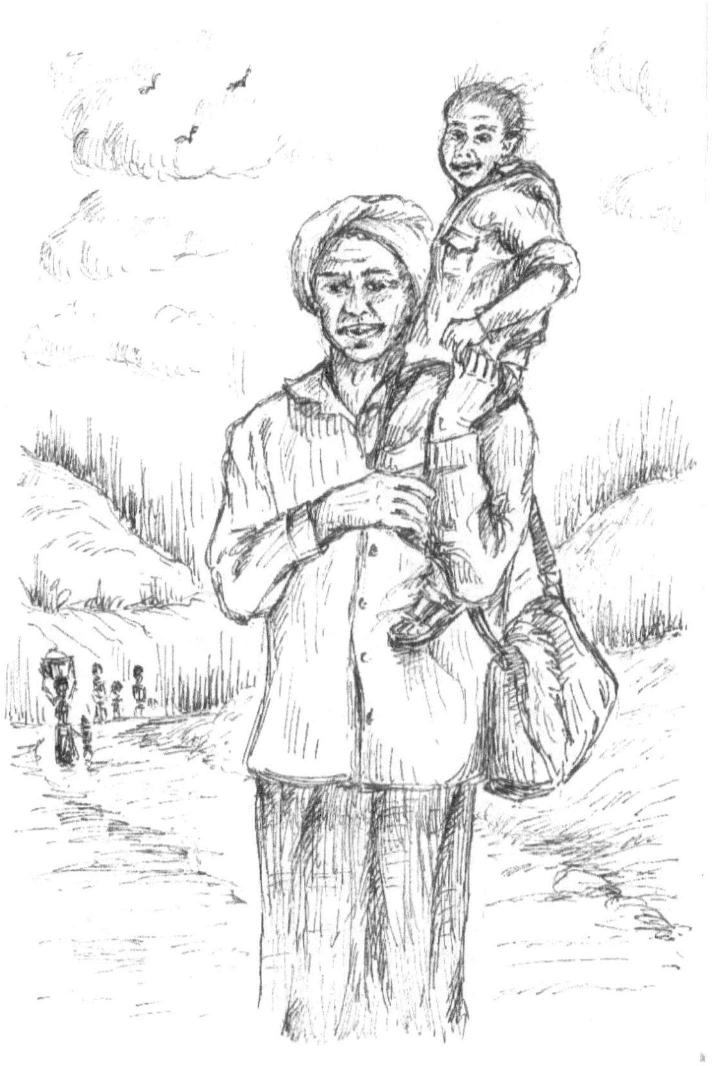

Share your Feedback

As an artist myself, I have always observed art as a manifestation of human culture. Just as culture varies significantly from one society to the other with a little shift in geography, even in our own country, so does art in its different forms and uniqueness. Thus the three entities are deeply inter-linked to each other.

Through my pencil sketches, I have tried to portray realistic flavors of a few sections of the society in different parts of India. My work will be successful only when it is capable to strike a chord with the emotional quotient of my readers.

Being a son of the soil to the "Cultural Capital" of India, Kolkata is woven around my soul. That is why my readers may find proportionately more anecdotes in and around the 'City of Joy'.

I shall remain thankful to all who may find some time to browse through my art-work showcased across my social media handles. I also wish to have all your valuable feedback and criticism, enabling me to offer you better work next time... Happy reading !!!

You are requested to kindly scan this code to access the online feedback form, for your easy access. Your valuable inputs will be of great help and motivation to me.

Thanks in advance

Indranil Mukherjee

Email: J4JISHUN@GMAIL.COM

Instagram: J4JISHUN

Twitter: J4JISHUN

Facebook: Indranil.Mukherjee.927